Hattuša

ege
YAYINLARI

DEUTSCHES ARCHÄOLOGISCHES INSTITUT
BOĞAZKÖY-EXPEDITION

HATTUSHA-GUIDE
A DAY IN THE HITTITE CAPITAL

BY JÜRGEN SEEHER

4. revised edition

EGE YAYINLARI

Ancient Anatolian Towns: 2

© 2011 Ege Yayınları and Jürgen Seeher
ISBN 978-605-5607-58-6

Graphic Design
Savaş Çekiç

Printed by
Paragraf Basım Sanayi A.Ş.
Yüzyıl Mah. Matbaacılar Sit. 2. Cadde No: 202/A Bağcılar, İstanbul
Tel: +90 (212) 629 06 07   Faks: +90 (212) 629 03 85
Sertifika No: 18469

Produced in Turkey by Ege Yayınları
Abdullah Sokak, No: 17, Taksim, 34433 İstanbul/Türkiye
Tel: +90 (212) 244 7521   Faks: +90 (212) 244 3209
E.posta: info@zerobooksonline.com
www.egeyayinlari.com

Welcome to Hattusha/Boğazköy!

As a visitor to the site you'll first want to know **what there is for you to see:**

From about 1650/1600 to 1200 BC, Hattusha was the Capital City of the Hittites, the head of an empire that reached across the broad lands of Anatolia, extending at times even into the north of Syria. The ruins of the city walls and the gates, the temples and the palaces awaiting the visitor today represent conditions in the 13th century BC, the zenith of the city. There had been, of course, earlier habitation in the region, and there was also substantial settlement here during the later "Phrygian", Hellenistic, Roman and Byzantine periods. Although there are not many remains from these periods to be seen, you will find information about them in this book.

In addition, a synopsis of the archaeological research at the site and a bibliography with suggestions for further reading are included at the end of the book.

Many finds from the excavations at Hattusha are on display in the Museum here at Boğazkale and at the Çorum Museum. It's well worth a visit!

The UNESCO (United Nations Educational, Scientific and Cultural Organization) keeps two registers of cultural monuments worth to be protected. Hattusha is included in both of them.

Since 1986 the ruins of the Hittite capital have been included as monument No. 377 in the World Heritage List (at present one of nine sites in Turkey): "Cultural and natural sites are present on this list. Its primary mission is to define and conserve the world's heritage, by drawing up a list of sites whose outstanding values should be preserved for all humanity. They constitute, together with many others, a common heritage, to be treasured as unique testimonies to an enduring past. Their disappearance would be an irreparable loss for each and every one of us. And yet, most are threatened, particularly in present times. The preservation of this common heritage concerns us all. The mission of this list is to ensure their protection througfh a closer co-operation among nations."
UNESCO

In 2001 the cuneiform tablet archives found at Hattusha, about 30.000 fragments now kept in the Museum of Anatolian Civilisations at Ankara and in the Archaeological Museums at Istanbul, were added to the Memory of the World List: "Documentary heritage reflects the diversity of languages, peoples and cultures. It is the mirror of the world and its memory. But this memory is fragile. Every day, irreplaceable parts of this memory disappear for ever. UNESCO has launched the Memory of the World Programme to guard against collective amnesia calling upon the preservation of the valuable archive holdings and library collections all over the world ensuring their wide dissemination."
UNESCO

Boğazköy/Hattusha has been declared a National Historical Park by the Turkish authorities in 1988.

Fig. 1 Hattusha from the air

A Day in Hattusha

On the Memory of the World List the ancient capital of the Hittites keeps company with famous cities such as Venice and Toledo, Jerusalem and Damascus, Rome and Carthage, Lübeck and Versailles, and Teotihuacan and Macchu Picchu.

You will find a general plan of the Hittite city Hattusha at the very back of this guide book. When speaking of the city, two districts are traditionally separated. The term **Lower City** refers to the district of the Old City of the Hittites. This stretched from

Fig. 2 The Lower City of Hattusha

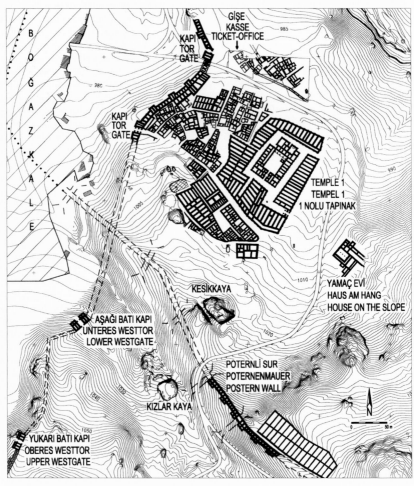

Fig. 3 Plan showing the structures excavated in the Lower City as well as the north end of the Upper City with its upper and lower West Gates

the outer northwestern wall at the edge of today's village up the slope to the southeast as far as the plateau known as Büyükkale, where the Royal Citadel of the Hittites stood. To the south and southwest the Lower City is bounded by the Postern Wall. The **Upper City**, then, denotes the district that grew up beyond this postern wall, extending southward to the summit at Yerkapı. It represents a newer part of the city.

Fig. 4 Please don't climb on the walls. We'd like them to survive for a few more millennia!

Reconstruction of the Mud Brick City Wall *(General Plan: No.2)*

At the starting point of a tour through Hattusha, one encounters the modern reconstruction of a 65 m long section of the city wall made of mud brick (Fig. 5). The reconstruction comprises three 7-8 m high sections of curtain walls and two 12-13 m high defence towers. It stands upon a section of the so-called "*Abschnittsmauer*" (dividing wall) of the Lower City. This inner city wall shielded the area of the Great Temple and adjacent settlement to the northwest (see General Plan at the back of the book). According to knowledge gained thus far, it was in use during the time of the Hittite empire (14th-13th century BC). The modern reconstruction of this stretch of wall gives an impression of how

Fig. 5 Reconstruction of the city wall, view from the north

well-fortified the ancient city was and the imposing effect it must have had upon visitors at that time. Furthermore, this reconstruction accentuates the fact that Hittite architecture was in essence brickwork. Sponsorship for this project was adopted by JT International.

Like all Hittite structures, the mud brick city walls were erected upon a stone socle, and - like all Hittite fortification walls - the c. 7 m thick *Abschnittsmauer* was built in the so-called 'box-system' (*Kastenmauer*): an outer and an inner wall (each c. 1.5-2 m thick) connected at regular intervals with transverse walls to form casemate-like spaces, which were filled with earth and stone rubble (Fig. 6). The walls were adjoined by towers built as separate constructions at intervals of 20-25 m (cp. Fig. 135). Thereby, the

Fig. 6 South curtain, constructing the brick wall in the 'box' system (Kastenmauer)

Fig. 7 Mud for making bricks is mixed in large shallow pits

junction of the towers with the fortification wall on the inner side is an even surface, while the towers protrude some 3-4 m from the front side of the wall.

Unfortunately, none of the original standing brickwork upon the stone socle is preserved anywhere in the remains of Hattusha's city walls. There are, however, clay models that date to the Hittite period, which served as a guide in reconstructing this particular wall (Fig. 70). For example, windows in the towers can be recognised in these models as well as the ends of wooden beams that protrude from the masonry. The triangular crenellation atop the city wall and the towers is especially typical.

Fig. 8 A mass of mud is formed in a wooden frame, the surface smoothed and then the frame removed

The brick needed for building walls was produced as follows. A mixture of clayey soil, straw and water was made in large pits (Fig. 7), whereby the straw was added as temper to prevent cracking during the time of drying. The bricks were shaped by putting a mass of the mixture into simple rectangular frames made of wood, the surface smoothed and the frame removed (Fig. 8). The bricks thus formed were then left in the sun to dry, which lasted about 10-12 days. Bricks produced in this manner measured 45x45x10 cm. This corresponds with the average size of Hittite mud bricks preserved in the burnt ruins at Hattusha. Thereby, one single brick weighs 34 kg. Approximately 64,000 bricks were produced for the reconstruction of the wall; together with the material for mortar and plaster this amounts to a total weight of nearly 2500 tons for the mud brick wall!

Fig. 9
View from the south
tower of the middle
portion of the cur-
tain and the north
tower

For reasons of security access to the Hittite city walls was
restricted. Only every sixth or seventh tower had a doorway,
through which the top of the wall could be reached from inside
the city. Therefore, only the reconstructed north tower has a stair-
way inside, whereas the ground floor of the south tower is solid.
The upper storey of both towers is accessible. Each tower has two
doors that lead to the curtain walls (Fig. 9). Following the models,
tall rectangular windows were reconstructed in the towers, not
only on the outer and inner sides, but also on the narrow sides
which protrude in front of the curtain wall. Access to the towers'
roof is gained by means of a ladder (Fig. 10).

In order to increase the stability of the tower storeys, an encir-
cling anchorage of large timbers (*Ringanker*) was emplaced directly

below the floors and the roof. The roof cover was made of a dense layer of poplar logs which was covered with a layer of mud. This was in turn covered with a 10-12 cm thick layer of *çorak*, an impermeable substance of earth, which was also used on the flat roofs of Hittite structures. The outer surface of the roof was divided into sections, each with a slight slope to enable rain water to be guided towards drains, which were made of timber halves. This kind of roofage demands constant care, as can still be observed today in villages in Anatolia. There after a heavy rainfall the roofs must be sealed anew with a cylinder and the slope of the surface controlled. Snow must be removed quickly, so that the melted water, which cannot flow off the sides, does not permeate the roof's covering.

Unfired mud bricks are a very sturdy building material, but they are sensitive to rain. Thus, a good plaster coating, that is always checked on and when necessary improved or renewed, is mandatory for their preservation. This covering or 'skin' preserves the material by diverting precipitation and by protecting against frost as well. The same mixture, without any modern preservatives, used for producing mud bricks and mortar was also employed for the plaster coating. The plaster was applied by hand only to the dampened brick walls in several stages (Fig. 11). The coating of plaster thus achieved does not have a flat surface, yet it is so thin that the underlying masonry is recognisable in an optically effective way.

The time required to produce the mud bricks and to erect the wall was almost eleven months, spanning three campaigns from 2003 to 2005. The reconstruction was not merely intended to render an optical impression of the original city wall (Fig. 12), but also to make a useful contribution to experimental archaeology. From the very beginning, all procedures in work, the work force employed, the length of time consumed in each stage of work and the amount of material used were documented exactly. In the coming years observations will be made as to how such a large structure made of unfired mud bricks will survive the raw climate of central Anatolia: What influence do the rays of the sun, rain, snow and frost exert upon the plaster surface, the roofage and the construction? In what intervals of time and to what extent are improvements necessary? Through these efforts more information will be gained concerning this kind of architecture, and with that not only the planning and execution of building, but also the problems of upkeep that were encountered by Hittite building constructors 3500 years ago can be apprehended.

Fig. 11 The wall of the south tower is covered with a plaster coating

Fig. 12 General view from the west

The Lower City *(General Plan: No.4)*

Large scale excavation has as yet only been undertaken within the **Lower Inner City** (Fig. 3). Today this part of the city is dominated by a large artificial platform on which **Temple 1,** in its time the grandest religious structure of the city, once stood. This temple complex was in use during the Empire period (14th-13th century BC), as do most of the **residences** here, the foundations of which you see just below (= north of) the temple terrace.

The domestic architecture of the Hittite lower city, which has changed frequently over the some four hundred years of the city's history, was typified by multi-room homes. In the earlier levels the **courtyard house** with an inner court open to the sky was the most popular; later the **vestibule house** with a roofed-over living area came into vogue. Priests, civil servants, merchants and artisans lived all together here while the farming community generally resided outside the city, in villages and hamlets scattered

Fig. 13 This is how Charles Texier, discoverer of Hattusha, found Temple 1 in 1834. The rocky ridge of Büyükkaya is rendered in the background

Fig. 14 Temple 1 and the Lower City

throughout the surroundings. The **house walls** were built of sundried mudbricks, partially supported by a timber frame construction, and the **flat roofs** were constructed of timbers covered with mud. These multi-room homes were equipped with ovens and open fireplaces for cooking; some even boasted **bathtubs** fashioned from clay (one such curiosity is on display in the Boğazkale Museum). While water for consumption and household use had to be carried from neighborhood fountains, many houses were equipped with a **drainage system** connected to sewage mains running beneath the streets and alleyways.

The oldest traces of settlement in the area of the Lower Inner City, however, go much further into the past. In the **Late Early Bronze Age** (end of the 3rd and beginning of the 2nd millennium BC) the area was settled by Hattians of local Anatolian origin, who called the locality Hattush. Remnants of an **Assyrian Merchants' Colony** of the 19th and 18th centuries BC have also been excavated here.

Fig. 15 Temple 1

Temple 1 *(General Plan: No.5)*

This temple, also known as **The Great Temple**, is the largest building structure in the city of Hattusha. The temple measures 65x42 m, and together with the storerooms that surround it, the temple complex covers an area of approximately 14,500 m². There is no dedicatory inscription, therefore the date of its erection is unknown; it is a fair assumption that it was in use during the Empire period. The entire complex stands on a terrace built up, no doubt, over still older structures of the Lower City.

Itinerary (the numbers refer to the plan Fig. 16): on the way from the parking lot to the temple, you first pass the **Lion Basin (1)**, which was originally some 5.5 m long, carved from a single block of limestone (Fig. 18a-b). The type of chisel marks on it tattle on the Byzantine or Roman stonemasons who cut the block into

Fig. 16   Plan of Temple 1:
1) the Lion Basin
2) the gateway to the Temple complex
3) the Green Stone
4) water basin
5) the Temple entrance
6) the Inner Court
7) altar (?)
8) stoa
9-10) the cult chambers
11) storerooms with large pottery vessels
12) the Street to the South Gate
13) the Southern District with the "House of Operations", and
14) the Grotto

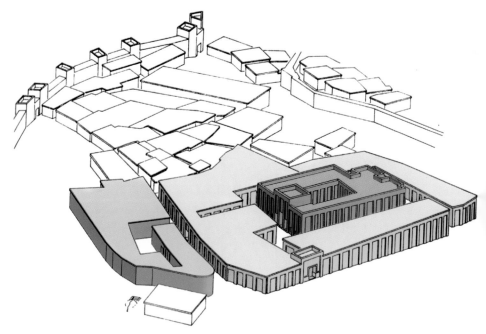

Fig. 17 Reconstruction of the three main parts of the Temple 1 complex: the temple proper (in red), the storage magazines (in yellow), and the Southern District with the "House of Operations" (in green) (after W. Schirmer)

pieces and hauled some of them away. The reconstruction drawing shows the four lions which once crouched at the four corners. Whether or not this monument actually served as a water basin is not really clear; it may well have been the base for a large statue.

The **gateway** (2) to the temple area, which you then pass through, has three large thresholds; here to the right and left you can still make out small rooms which must have provided shelter for the temple guards. Once past the gateway you are now on the paved **Street of the Temple**, which takes you past the storerooms and which surrounds the central temple building. In one of the storerooms on the left you will come upon the **Green Stone** (3), embroiled in many, many tales (Fig. 19).

Fig. 18a The millennia have left their traces on the Lion Basin

Fig. 18b The Lion Basin once featured crouching lions at all four corners
(Reconstruction by O. Puchstein, 1912)

Fig. 19 The Green Stone in one of the storerooms of Temple 1

The Green Stone arrived here neither from Egypt nor as a meteor from outer space. Nor has its power to bring riches or children to those who touch it yet been proven. It may well have played a role in some religious cult, but which one we have no idea. Although sacred stones are mentioned in the Hittite texts, not a single one is explicitly described as being green. What we have here is a block of green nephrite-type stone common in the geology of the region. The Stone must have once stood elsewhere, for it lies beneath the original surface of the temple storeroom, as its level in comparison to the nearby doorway clearly demonstrates. A similar – if smaller and not so carefully worked – green stone has also been found in a structure near Temple 5 in the Upper City.

A small **water basin** (4) chiseled from a limestone block may well have served in cult ritual (Fig. 20). Carefully worked limestone blocks also form the striking wall socles that often still stand to their original height of 1.5 m (Figs. 21-22). Some of the blocks are up to five meters in length and weight 20 tons or more. The **walls** themselves are no longer to be seen, for like the walls of the other structures in the Hittite city, they too were of a massive **timber frame construction** filled with mudbrick (Fig. 23). They were then covered with a layer of mud plaster, in areas worked into designs in relief and most probably also rather lavishly painted. Such ornamentation has been attested in other buildings of Hattusha. The **roof** of the Great Temple consisted of a ceiling of timbers sealed with mud. The many **dowel holes** seen on the surfaces of the limestone blocks (Fig. 24) enabled the builders to fix the upper wall onto the blocks with dowels of wood and

Fig. 20 Basin along the paved road leading to the Temple

Fig. 21 The paved Temple Street with storage magazines

Fig. 22 Temple 1. The large courtyard, too, was originally paved with large stone slabs

bronze. In the stone socle of the Great Temple alone there are hundreds and hundreds of such dowel holes produced by drilling.

The Temple Building. Because there is no staircase, the temple itself must have consisted of only one story – although probably with a much higher ceiling than those of the residences. The **entrance (5)** to the temple proper was in the narrow end to the southwest (Figs. 22 and 25). On the large stone blocks of the **threshold** you can still see where the doors pivoted at the corners, as well as traces of abrasion where the heavy **wooden doors** swung open and closed. Beyond is the 27x20 m **inner court (6)**, beyond which lay the chambers of the actual sanctuary. The court, open to the sky, was surrounded by high walls and paved with large flat stones (some of which are preserved in the eastern –the back right– corner). Although today the court makes rather

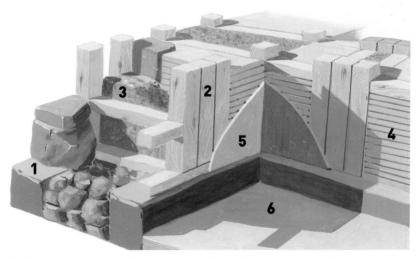

Fig. 23 Reconstruction of the walls in Temple 1: 1) foundation and socle of stone blocks, 2) timber framework, 3) fill of earth and stones, 4) mudbricks, 5) wall plaster, and 6) lime-plastered floor on a layer of packed earth (U. Betin, after P. Neve)

Fig. 24 The wall socle with dowel holes for support of the wooden framework

The Principle of the Hittite Drill. The first step was to secure a wooden frame over the place where the hole was to be drilled. A short bronze tube was then positioned in the frame at right angles to the surface. The tube could then be spun very quickly in position with the aid of a cord wrapped around it; two workers would pull the cord back and forth in a sawing motion. With water and sand used as an abrasive, it was possible to drill neat cylindrical holes relatively quickly. Experiment has demonstrated that a hole about 3.5 cm across could be drilled at the rate of 6-8 cm (depth) per hour. The stone core left by the tube was then simply struck out with a blow; stubs of the cores can be seen in many of the holes.

a drab impression, we know from the Hittite texts that most celebrations took place in the temple courtyards; with a little imagination you should be able to picture the court milling with brightly dressed onlookers and brightened by standards and pennants, the air filled with music and incense. The cuneiform tablets of the Hittites describe such ceremonies in detail.

Crossing the court, you will see the socle of a **freestanding construction** (7) that may have been an altar. Rather than limestone, gabbro was used, a hard greenish black igneous rock that was also employed for the column bases of an **open stoa** (8) along the opposite end of the court. It was through this portico and several antechambers that the King and Queen – as the High Priests of the Land – and a few select temple priests could reach the innermost

Fig. 25 The Temple entrance (the entrance to the court) was flanked by small rooms for the guards

sanctuary, the Holy of Holies; admission was permitted only to them. The fact that there are two **cult chambers (9 and 10)** here indicates that the temple was **a twin temple** dedicated to two deities. Considering the size of the temple, it is only appropriate that the two most important deities of the Land were honored here: **the Weather God of Hatti and the Sun Goddess of Arinna.**

The Cult Chambers. The greenish black stone gabbro was also used for the socles of the cult chambers. The blocks were fitted together exactly, in some places even interlocking. Whereas only the foundations of the western chamber to the left (**No. 9**) remain, nearly the entire socle of the eastern chamber to the right (**No. 10**) is still preserved; it measures 8x10 m. A cult statue would have stood on the large block against the far end of the

Fig. 26 Cult chamber with base for the cult statue

room (Fig. 26). Large windows, reaching nearly to the floor (the low sills are quite apparent) on the left and right, as well as on the side walls would have illuminated the room well when need be; they were probably usually closed with wooden shutters to preserve the sanctity of the place.

Other rooms in the temple could also have been used for rituals; they also served as dressing rooms for the priests and storage for cult paraphernalia. They were unfortunately mostly empty when discovered, as were the 82 ground-floor **rooms of the long storage magazines** which surrounded the temple. The only finds left were huge **pottery vessels (11)** sunk into the ground, some of which are still in place (Fig. 30). The remains of hundreds of such vessels were found in the long narrow storerooms along

Fig. 27 Thresholds of the storeroom doors

Fig. 28 Gutter to drain water from the Inner Court

28

Fig. 29 Storerooms along the northwest side of Temple 1

the northwestern aisle. They held up to 2000 liters apiece and provided **storage for the temple provender,** which must have included cereal grains, dried beans and the like, oil and wine. Many of the vessels had symbols scratched onto their shoulders, obviously indication of the contents and their designated purpose. The contents of the storerooms along the aisle on the opposite side of the temple were different; thousands of **cuneiform tablets** and fragments were found here, fallen from the wooden shelves on which they were once arranged like archives.

Large monolithic **doorsills** mark the position of doorways between the storage rooms (Fig. 27). The 82 rooms we can count around the temple today represent only the ground floor; some of these storage depots were originally two and perhaps –in places–

Fig. 30 Large vessels in the storerooms of Temple 1

three-storied, with stairwells providing access to the upper floors. We can thus estimate that these storage magazines surrounding the temple contained a max. total of around 200 storerooms.

The street (12) and the Southern District (13). A paved street running along the southwestern side of the temple led downward to the opening in the inner city wall known as the **South Gate**, and under the street ran the sewage canal serving this part of the city. Across the street in this so-called Southern District a 5,300 m^2 walled-in building complex (also known as Complex 1) has been excavated. The single entrance in the circuit wall stands directly opposite the side entrance to the temple precinct. In addition to

The temple magazines with so many storerooms provided space for all the paraphernalia that might be needed for cult rituals and parades: dishes of pottery and metal; tables, chairs and other pieces of furniture; carts; musical instruments; raiment and robes for priests, priestesses and assistants; and probably much, much more, including – at least temporarily – even live animals for sacrifice.

There must also have been offices, for the temples played a role in the economy as well; bookkeeping and bureaucracy would have been unavoidable. There were special archives for such documents, which were written on wooden rosters coated with wax. One could even hold down a job as a "wood-roster scribe". These archives have irretrievably vanished.

Fig. 31 Spring grotto above the Southern District near Temple 1

storerooms and cult chambers the complex may have included workshops as well; unfortunately it was completely cleared out when the city was deserted, leaving us very little in the way of clues to its function. A cuneiform tablet found here mentions a E-GISH-KINTI, that is, a "House of Operations", tasks in which priests, musicians, singers, and both clay tablet and wood-roster scribes –among others– were involved. If this concept of a work area applies to the complex as a whole, it must have included workshops and ateliers as well as perhaps living space for the official personnel of the Great Temple.

A small walled **grotto (14)**, in which the water from a spring collected, lay just above the "House of Operations" (Fig. 31). The lintel above the entrance, only partially preserved (here restored; the original is in the Boğazkale Museum), was decorated in relief. A stele found in the debris of the precinct (now kept in the Museum of Anatolian Civilizations at Ankara) bore a hieroglyphic inscription which indicates that the spring and grotto had religious significance.

– End of Round Tour in the Great Temple –

The House on the Slope *(General Plan:* No.6)

The steep slope that rises from the Great Temple to the Royal Citadel of Büyükkale was also a part of the Old City of the Hittites, which by the 16th century BC must have been encircled by a fortification wall. On the slope there were a variety of terraced buildings that sat on or nestled between the rocky outcroppings. The so-called House on the Slope is a particularly monumental example (Figs. 32-33). Two-storied and most impressive in size, 32x36 m, it must not have been a private house, but a **building of administrative function.** This concept is supported by the **grand hall,** 13x17 m, reconstructed on the upper floor. Housekeeping and storage was relegated to the lower floor,

Fig. 32 The House on the Slope, with Büyükkaya in the background

Fig. 33 The House on the Slope, reconstructed (U. Betin, after R. Naumann)

where a copious **collection of clay tablets** was found during excavation.

Towards the end of the 13th century BC the House on the Slope was destroyed by fire and never again rebuilt. The well-fired mudbrick walls against the slope at the back are still standing; as protection against the elements, however, they have been reinforced with a thick outer casing.

Kesikkaya *(General Plan: No.7)*

South of the Great Temple, to the right as you climb towards the Upper City, a striking outcropping of rock will catch your eye (Fig. 34). The wide cleft that splits the rock into two is natural. The early excavators, anticipating the existence of a royal grave here, carefully cleaned the chasm out in 1911 only to be

Fig. 34 The rock outcropping of Kesikkaya

disappointed. There must once have been a Hittite structure atop the rock, however, for step-like ledges accompanied by rows of bore-holes climb the side facing the valley. The Hittites most likely also helped themselves to the rock as convenient building material; at least part of the limestone used in the Lower City and the temple precinct must have come from here. From the street you can see scars high up on the rock; these, however, are from Roman and Byzantine quarrying. It may be from these scars that the cliff takes its name (Kesikkaya means "cut rock"); it may be from the large cleft below.

The Postern Wall *(General Plan: No.8)*

Shortly beyond Kesikkaya the street curves to the left, cutting through **the oldest fortifications of Hattusha.** Since the 16th century BC this wall protected the Old City of the Hittites – the Lower City – on the south and southwest. Following the natural line of the valley, the fortifications led all the way up to the Royal Citadel of Büyükkale. What you first notice from the street is the earthen wall on which the fortress stood. Like nearly all Hittite walls, this too was built as a **casemate wall,** that is to say it consisted of sturdy inner and outer walls divided at regular intervals by crosswalls. The interior "rooms" were then packed full of earth. The total width, then, was nearly eight meters, and along its length towers were built at intervals of 12 to 20 meters.

Fig. 35 Entrance to one of the posterns (= tunnels) in the Postern Wall

Fig. 36
One of the posterns
not accessible today
during excavation

Eight tunnels, or **posterns** led underneath the wall to openings outside (Figs. 35-36). They are between 70 and 180 m distant from one another. You can see the entrances today, although the passages are filled with debris. The tunnels were of **corbeled masonry** like the passageway in the Upper City at Yerkapı, which you can walk through during your visit. The function of these posterns remains open to interpretation. Their earlier identification as sally ports, through which one could run out and attack the besieging enemy from the rear, gave rise to the name postern, from the Latin *posterula* (= back or side door). There must, however, be more behind this phenomenon, for certainly the Hittites would have better camouflaged sally ports.

On a clay tablet found in the cuneiform archives of Hattusha, King Hantili, the third king of the Old Empire period, reports that he built fortifications for Hattusha, which "earlier had no protection whatsoever". Reigning in the 16th century BC, King Hantili must certainly have been exaggerating a bit, or perhaps he was implying that the earlier defense system was nothing in comparison to his much stronger city wall. The Postern Wall probably belonged to the king's new defenses. Over the following centuries the Postern Wall was then renovated and remodeled.

Grain Silo of the Old Hittite Period
(General Plan: No.8a)

In the Old Hittite Period, a huge subterranean grain silo was erected behind the postern wall, half way between Kızlar Kaya and Büyükkale. The remains of this complex lie buried under up to 7 m of soil debris and are not accessible.

This building structure is approximately 118 m long (longer than a soccer field!) and 30 to 40 m wide (Fig. 37). It consists of two rows of 16 compartments each; the walls are made of mud brick tiles and about 1,5 m thick. The exterior walls were insulated on the outside with thick layers of clay, to keep moisture out.

The storage of grain in these self-contained compartments is based on the same principle as with the earth-silos on Büyükkaya (ref. Fig. 137): The compartments were lined with a thick layer of straw and then filled up to the rim with grain. On top came

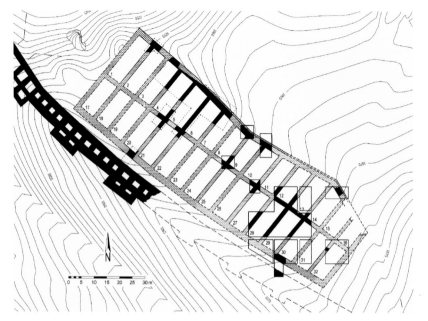

Fig. 37 Plan of the subterranean silo complex of the Old Hittite period with the excavated areas indicated; the postern wall passes by on the left side

another layer of straw and then a thick layer of loamy soil. Thus sealed hermetically, the grain could be kept for many years. Thanks to this method of storage, a part of this grain has been preserved until the present day: At some time during the 16th century BC, a fire broke out in the silo complex and destroyed twelve of the compartments (Fig. 38). The fire travelled from one room to the next consuming the wooden beams within the upper parts of the walls, but due to a lack of oxygen the grain did not burn completely. Instead, much of it was charred, just like the logs in a charcoal-pile. This resulted in grain layers more than one meter thick that were preserved in some of the compartments (Fig. 39) – a singular find in the Ancient Near East.

Fig. 38 Southeastern part of the silo complex with burnt mud brick walls

41

Fig. 39 1,2 m thick layer of charred grain in one of the silo compartments

Botanical analysis has shown that mostly barley was stored in this silo. In some compartments, however, wheat (Einkorn) was kept. Mixed with the charred grain there is a striking lot of seeds of other food plants and weeds; they once came in from the fields together with the grain harvest (Fig. 40). These finds supply further information for the reconstruction of the ancient environment.

Fig. 40
The close-up view of a sample of charred seeds shows a variety of species

The actual height of the compartments in the silo is not known; statements concerning the capacity therefore have to remain vague – a figure between 7.000 and 9.000 cubic meters of grain seems realistic. This amount corresponds to the annual supply for 20.000-30.000 people. It has to be kept in mind, however, that barley was also used as fodder and for brewing beer. In any case, due to its enormous size it seems clear that this was not only a reserve for the city Hattusha - this silo formed part of the state treasury and thus of the economic power the Hittite Great King could rely on.

Kızlar Kaya *(General Plan: No.9)*

In the valley beyond the Postern Wall and to the right of the street is the Kızlar Kaya (= The Maidens' Rock; Fig. 41). According to an old story there was once a picture or relief of a young girl on the rock face. Since the beginning of the 20th century

Fig. 41 The small rocky plateau of Kızlar Kaya

– at least – no one has reported seeing it. Although Roman/
Byzantine masons at work here removed stone blocks, the basic
configuration of the site stems from Hittite times. There is a rock
platform with various cuttings and bench-like projections that
may well have been part of a former structure. Most striking
are the chiseled stump-like projections rising from the floor of the
platform; they remind one of altars.

The Lower and Upper West Gates
(General Plan: Nos.10 and 11)

Both of these city gates are located along the western stretch of
the fortification wall of the Upper City (Figs. 42-43). Both display
two doorways originally built as parabolic arches, flanked by
towers. In each doorway there used to be a pair of huge wooden
doors which swung open toward the interior on pivots set in the
large stone sockets. They thus match the two great city gates in the
southern curve of the wall enclosing the Upper City, the Lion and
the King's Gate, save that these in the north boast no sculptural
ornament. The **Lower West Gate** is visible from the street, that is,
past the Kızlar Kaya to the northwest. It must stand just over a path
which – hundreds of years before this wall was ever built – led up
out of the valley nearly parallel to the postern wall you see today.
The **Upper West Gate,** on the other hand, lay further uphill out of
sight from the street. It served as an entrance to the high ridge in
the west of the new city, a district not yet archaeologically explored.

Fig. 42 The Lower West Gate

Fig. 43 The Upper West Gate

TOUR THROUGH THE UPPER CITY

Shortly past Kızlar Kaya the way forks; to make a **circular tour** it is best to take the right-hand path which maeanders its way into the Upper City of Hattusha (Fig. 44). This district to the west and south of the Postern Wall was perhaps enclosed during the period of the Hittite Empire by the stretch of city wall about 3.3 km long which we see here today. As you can see on the plan, the asphalt road runs along at some distance below the western city wall. The area here, also called the western Upper City, is currently under archaeological investigation.

Fig. 44 The Upper City of Hattusha

Fig. 45 The rock of Sarıkale dominates the western part of the Upper City

Sarıkale *(General Plan: No.12)*

The cliffs of Sarıkale (=Yellow Fortress), rising some 60 m up out of the valley, visually dominate the city landscape (Fig. 45). This rocky spur was built over with **an extensive architectural complex** in Hittite times (Fig. 46). Remains of masonry, beddings cut into the rock to receive the great stone blocks and a cistern (with remains of a corbeled vault) are preserved. It could be approached only from the back (the SE side), where ruins of a gate and a fortification wall with bastions have survived. There can be no doubt that the structure on this impressive cliff nearly in the center of the Upper City had a very special function. The

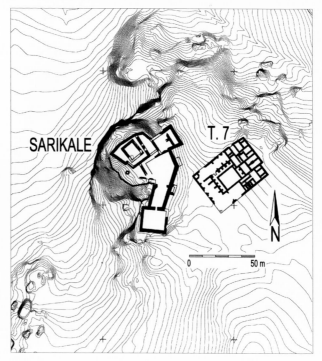

Fig. 46 To the east, on a gentle slope behind Sarıkale lies
Temple 7 (13th century BC)

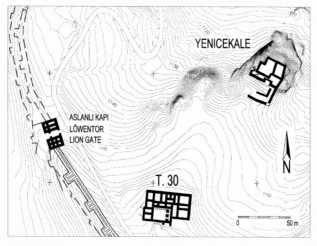

Fig. 47 Not far from the Lion Gate you see Temple 30 on a low rise
and the building complex of Yenicekale on a rocky peak

expression "**rock-crest houses**" recurs several times in Hittite texts connected with cults, most especially with the cult of the dead. These passages may well refer to structures like those on Sarıkale, Yenicekale and Nişantaş, constructions which indeed stood on separate rock outcroppings.

The Hittite remains on Sarıkale have been greatly diminished both by erosion and by later activity on the cliffs; in **Byzantine times** the complex was reused and more fortifications built. It may have been the palace of the dignitary who ruled over the sizable Byzantine settlement on the saddle to the southeast of Sarıkale.

The Lion Gate *(General Plan: No.13)*

After a last hairpin bend the road takes you directly up to the fortifications at the southwest of the Upper City. Here stands the Lion Gate, one of the two grand entrances in the southern curve of the city wall of Hattusha (Fig. 47-49). Most certainly it was originally designed for wheeled transport as well; the step inside the gate is modern. As with all the larger city gates, two rectangular **towers** (each about 15x10 m in plan) flanked the actual entranceway, or passage between the exterior and interior portals. The walls of this vestibule-like **entranceway** were built of huge blocks. Both portals were fitted with pairs of heavy **wooden doors,** those at the exterior most probably sheathed in bronze. Of the original **pivot stones** into which the wings of the two double doors were hinged, only one – toward the inside of the right-hand block at the exterior doorway – can still be seen. The corresponding sockets at the King's Gate are better preserved.

Fig. 48 The Lion Gate

Fig. 49 The computer reconstruction of the Lion Gate shows how massive and forbidding the big city gates of Hattusha once looked (H. Schriever)

"When they lift the copper bolts of the door in the morning – your son or your servant, whomever you have sent – if the seal on the door should 'move,' then 'an official of Hatti' or a commanding officer or whatever other 'official' is on duty must also inspect the seal and open the door accordingly. The copper bolt should then, however, be returned to your house and put back in its place". These were the instructions given to a mayor of the city of Hattusha by the Great King Arnuwanda, as found inscribed on a cuneiform tablet. In other words, the doors were barred and sealed in the evenings, and each morning before the doors were opened, there was an official check that the sealing was still intact.

Both of the doors could be closed from inside; the wings were then barred with massive **wooden bolts.** Holes to receive these bolts can be seen beside the outer portal in the side wall of the vestibule.

The door takes its name from the two **sculptured lions** whose heads, breasts and feet were cut out of the exterior of the huge blocks lining the passageway (Figs. 50-51). Lions were popular figures of protection and ornament at doorways throughout the ancient Near East, and Hattusha was no exception; lions guarded not only this gate, but several temple entrances and the portals to the Royal Palace as well. All were most vividly depicted, their teeth clenched, their tongues hanging from their mouths, and their wide eyes alert and threatening. The eyeballs were originally inlaid with a white limestone fill set with black pupils. A **computer**

Fig. 50 The head of the lion to the right as it appeared in 1907; unfortunately it was later damaged

Fig. 51 Still a majestic sight after more than three millenia!

Fig. 52
The lions' paws stand
on separate
stone blocks

Fig. 53
The locks of
the lion's mane

reconstruction recreates the general impression of the exterior of the gate in its former glory (Fig. 49). Here one is immediately struck by the **parabolic form** of the entrance, typical of many Hittite portals and gateways.

The **mastery of the carving** is most apparent on the surviving head of the lion to the right, but is clear as well in the princely mane and the detail in the front paws (Figs. 52-53). The feet stand on separate blocks, on the surfaces of which can be seen bowl-like depressions. It may be that offerings were left here, but unfortunately we have not yet encountered any proof of this from Hittite texts.

The head of the **lion on the left,** which was clearly larger than his partner, had already been broken away in antiquity. It has been reconstructed in 2011. Here, above at the left – at midday in

Fig. 54-55   The Hieroglyphic inscription to the upper left of the left-hand lion

Fig. 56 Polygonal masonry in the exterior of the tower left of the Lion Gate

proper light – you can just make out a luvian **hieroglyphic inscription** (Figs. 54-55). The name of the gate must have been written here, for at the very bottom of the inscription stands the character for "gate".

The **exterior façade of the left tower** constitutes a fine example of the skills of the Hittite master mason (Fig. 56). Still preserved to a height of 4.6 m, the tower is built in **polygonal masonry** employing massive limestone blocks. Although earthquakes have nudged some of them slightly out of position, others remain so tightly in place that you cannot even insert a sheet of paper between them. The front surfaces of the limestone blocks toward the top of the façade are irregular, and some protrude awkwardly from the face of the wall. This tells us that the first surfaces of the blocks to be worked were those that fit against the masonry under

Fig. 57 The Lion Gate from the air

and beside them; only after the blocks were securely in place, was the façade trimmed and smoothed. For some reason or other this final task was neglected here on the face of the tower.

The **external approach** to the Lion Gate (Fig. 57) was a ramp leading steeply upward from the south alongside the fortification wall. Across the ramp on the valley side was a second stretch of defense wall with its own tower. Thus an assailant approaching the gate would have had to pass through a **narrow alleyway** where he would have been attacked from two sides before he could ever reach the gate itself. The outer wall here at the Lion Gate is too poorly preserved to illustrate this layout of the defenses, but the reconstruction at the King's Gate (Figs. 100-101) demonstrates it clearly.

Fig. 58 The building complex on Yenicekale as idealized by Charles Texier, 1839

Fig. 59 Yenicekale

Temple 30 and Yenicekale

(General Plan: Nos.14 and 15)

The street now proceeds directly along the wall upwards from the Lion Gate to the highest point of the city. To the left are the restored foundations of **Temple 30**, which lie by themselves on a low rise near the Lion Gate (Fig. 47). The structure, about 30x40 m, reflects the usual temple plan with a large inner courtyard. Only the foundations remain, for after the destruction of the temple, its ruins served both as a quarry and as foundations for several houses and workshops fitted out with potters' kilns.

Below this temple – some 150 m northeast of the Lion Gate – you see the complex of **Yenicekale** atop a rock platform (Figs. 58-59). The summit of the natural rocky outcropping here was leveled and the lateral precipices built up to form an artificial platform for the building complex. The well preserved circuit wall, still standing to a good seven meters, elicits a healthy respect for the art of the Hittite engineers; some of the large limestone blocks in the wall weigh at least two or three tons!

On top of the artificial plateau measuring ca. 25x28 m are a small cistern and the remnants of foundations for walls, giving little clue as to the original purpose of the complex here. Although the complex of Yenicekale is much smaller than that of Sarıkale, it brings the same question to mind. Could this have been one of the "rock-crest houses" mentioned in the Hittite texts?

The Southern Ponds *(General Plan: No.16)*

On your way from the Lion Gate up to Yerkapı you can see on your left hand a spur in the terrain which protrudes about 200 m northward into the area of the Upper City. Aerial photographs revealed two long depressions side by side on the flat upper surface of this spur (Fig. 62, at the left). They belong to large water basins built by the Hittites probably as early as the 15. century BC. The basins were narrow, in order to reduce the loss through evaporation, but up to 8 m deep. Since the marly ground here is completely watertight, there was no need for further insulation of the embankments. The plan and the computer reconstruction (Fig. 60-61) show five basins, located at practically the highest point within the city. Water was probably collected from springs situated a little higher near Yerkapı, and perhaps also by means of clay pipelines and canals from the southern hinterland of the city. Again by means of clay pipelines, water could be sent from here to almost everywhere in the city – these must represent ponds which served as city water reservoirs. Here one may ask why the ancient engineers built five small basins instead of one or two large ones. The answer is "risk management": Like with the Eastern Ponds in the Upper City (Fig. 102-103; General Plan No. 24), water was distributed to several separate basins; in case of a break in the embankment or pollution of some kind, only a part but not all of the water reserve was lost.

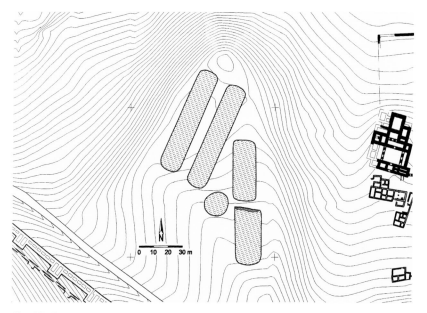

Fig. 60 Plan of the Southern Ponds in the Upper City

Fig. 61 The computer reconstruction gives an idea how the Southern Ponds may have looked like

Fig. 62 Aerial view of the rampart at Yerkapı; behind it, the Temple District in the Upper City

The Rampart of Yerkapı *(General Plan: No.17)*

The highest and southernmost point in the city fortifications is marked by the articificial ridge of Yerkapı (Figs. 62-63; 66-67). The city wall, which arches up toward the summit from the Lion Gate in the west and the King's Gate in the east, crowns the ridge, with the Sphinx Gate located just at the center. We recommend a walk which takes you first through the postern tunnel and to your left (= east) along the outside of the rampart. Steps at the east end will then bring you back up the slope to the Sphinx Gate, through which you can re-enter the city and return to your starting point here.

The great rampart takes its name Yerkapı (= gate in the earth) from the only **postern** which you can actually walk through today in Hattusha. The tunnel itself was built before the construction of

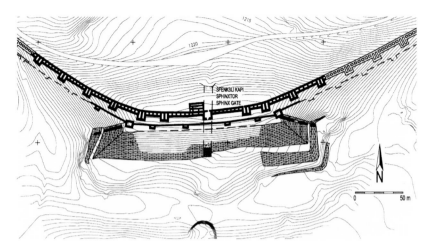

Fig. 63 The rampart of Yerkapı at the southern edge of the city. The postern leads through the rampart directly under the Sphinx Gate (at center)

Fig. 64 The postern of Yerkapı

the great earthen rampart. An example of **corbeled masonry**, the tunnel walls were laid with each successive course of huge limestone blocks protruding a bit further inward, forming a pointed vault, closed at the top by wedge-shaped keystones (Fig. 64). The construction is especially stable because each of the long blocks in the side walls protrudes deep into the earthen fill covering the tunnel.

Fig. 65 The exterior gate of the postern at Yerkapı, with the Sphinx Gate above

Fig. 66 The Yerkapı rampart from the southwest

Fig. 67 The white-paved embankment constituted a landmark visible from afar

Fig. 68 On either side, narrow staircases led to the top of the Yerkapı rampart

The passage, 3 to 3.3 m high, is 71 m long and slopes notice-ably downward as it exits from the city. The floor was covered with a **white coating** that reflected some of the scant light from the ends to allow limited visibility. **Both ends of the passage** were originally fitted with **double-winged wooden doors.** While the doorway facing the city was set into the slope of the earthen rampart, the exit on the exterior was reinforced by a massive construction which can be seen from far and wide (Fig. 65). This construction alone made the passage unsuitable for a sally-port through which one could surprise the enemy by falling on his rear. The fact that this gate was not planned for defense is also reflect-ed in its distance from the fortress walls above: the long-range weapon used by the Hittites was a bow and arrow with accuracy only within a distance of 50-60 meters; sharpshooters atop the wall would not have been able to provide effective cover for their comrades exiting below.

The great rampart (250 m long on a foundation a good 80 m across) stands some 30 m high on **the exterior,** which was – in contrast to the interior – **paved with a layer of stone** (Figs. 66-67). The whole of the exterior must have originally been covered; the stones in the upper part, bare today, were put to secondary use in the construction of an outer wall with towers atop it. **Gutters** for drainage carried rainwater from the crown of the rampart down the side of this 'paved' slope at intervals of about 21 meters.

At either end of the stone-covered slope a **steep flight of steps** (Fig. 68) led up to the crown, still another proof that this wall was not constructed mainly on the principle of defense. Well trained

Fig. 69 A reconstruction of the final phase of the Yerkapı rampart showing the main and exterior fortification walls (P. Neve)

soldiers, moreover, could certainly have clambered up the slope here at a run; it rises at an angle of only 35 degrees. At any rate, an enemy force would not likely have chosen to storm the city from here when only a short distance to the right and the left the wall below the defense circuit was considerably lower. The paved rampart must have been erected primarily as an **architectural monument**, a manifestation of the city's might and/or religious significance. From afar the high ridge with its crown of city walls and towers would have gleamed white in the landscape, an impressive landmark to travelers and guests approaching from the south (Fig. 69).

The City Wall on the Ridge of Yerkapı

After you have climbed the stairs (a total of 102 steps at the east, 81 at the west!) you will be in a position to have a close look at the **Hittite fortification wall** itself. As to be expected it is a casemate wall with massive inner and outer walls connected by crosswalls at regular intervals. Nowhere, unfortunately, is there a full-standing example of a Hittite defense wall, so we can only postulate the height. The lower part, probably 1-2 m high, was of stone masonry; upon this sat a structure of mudbrick. Perhaps another 5-7 m high, the latter incorporated battlements and a corridor for defense. The towers, which added still more height, were also of mudbrick.

Fortunately there are clay representations of city fortifications decorating the rims of large pottery vessels (Fig. 70); these give us some impression of the appearance of the Hittite fortifications. We know from these, for example, that the walls and towers were crowned with **triangular crenellations** (see also p. 6-13).

Fig. 70 Fragment of a Hittite vessel (15th/14th century BC) shaped like a fortress tower. Detail indicates even the ends of the wooden beams protruding from the mudbrick structure

Originally there was only a single line of fortifications across the ridge of Yerkapı. Later it apparently became necessary to reinforce the defenses with an **exterior auxiliary wall**. Two towers of the main wall were dismantled at this time, and stones robbed from the paving on the slope. This wall on the exterior now blocked off use the staircases at either end, and the Sphinx Gate at the center must have lost its function as well. Obviously, defense of the city had become the foremost criterion; the date would have been in the 13th century BC, when the Empire was already headed into decline.

The Sphinx Gate *(General Plan: No.18)*

At the middle of the stretch of city wall across the artificial ridge of Yerkapı stands the Sphinx Gate. In contrast to the other grand city gates, it is not flanked by towers, but passes directly through a tower. It takes its name from the **four sculpted sphinxes** that once adorned the great blocks on either side of the doorways. Sphinxes are heterogenous creatures with a human head and the body of a lion. The Hittites must have adopted the sphinx from Egypt, where the Sphinx represented a King. The soft facial contours of Hittite sphinxes, however, suggest that they represent females.

Today only the sphinx at the west of the exterior doorway remains in position (Fig. 71). The front of the body has been sculpted from head to foot in the round on the exterior of the large block. Although the breast and face are broken away, similar sculpture found at other locations allows us to reconstruct the face of a person wearing a headdress (cf. Fig. 113). It is this in

Fig. 71

Fig. 72 The outer doorway of the Sphinx Gate

When you reach the Sphinx Gate, glance downward to the south. Here you see a hollow; from here came most of the soil with which the artificial ridge was built. Beyond you see a wood (Fig. 72), thanks to the former excavator of the site Peter Neve. At the beginning of the 1980s this area was indistinguishable from the other barren crests within the horizon; with the permission of the Turkish Forestry Service, this area was fenced off. This simple precaution protected the scrub oak so profuse in the environs from being nibbled off by the free-wandering herds of pasturing goats, and the scrub has grown into actual trees. With the exception of a few pines along the periphery of the hollow, not a single tree has been planted here! As your eyes wander across the treetops rustling in the breeze, you have at least a glimpse of what the landscape here must have looked like in former times.

Fig. 73 The interior façade of the Sphinx Gate when exposed in 1907

particular which suggests the **Egyptian influence**. Such a headdress is portrayed on the heads of the pharaohs and reflected in the hairdressing of Hathor, goddess of heaven and love. The lower edge of the hood-like headdress or coiffure fell to the shoulders, where it ended in a curve or a curl. **Rosettes** on the head are clustered into a bough-like embellishment.

The block with the **second outer sphinx** is completely missing, most probably pulled from its position and carried off to be used as building material elsewhere. It seems that the same fate was in store for the block with the remaining sphinx. It was found dismantled and broken into pieces outside the gate; on the reverse of the block were found the deep chiseled grooves typical of the Roman and Byzantine stonemasons' procedure when splitting large blocks into smaller ones. From this block we can also tell that the doorway of the Sphinx Gate was not parabolic in form like those of the other city gates; it was a simple rectangle formed with a horizontal lintel above.

This outer doorway featured **a door with two wings**. On the threshold you can see the sockets where the doors were hinged.

The **doorway opening into the city**, on the other hand, stood open; there were no doors at the interior of the entranceway. **Two sculpted sphinxes** originally flanked the doorway here as well, gazing out over the city within the walls. In the heat of the fire that destroyed the tower here, the limestone statues crackled and split (Fig. 73). The sculpted blocks were in such poor condition by the time of the 1907 excavations that it was necessary to remove them to a sheltered environment in order to restore them. Today the sphinx from the west side of the interior doorway (Fig. 74) stands on display in the Near Eastern Museum in Istanbul, and the right-hand sphinx (Fig. 75) in the Near Eastern Museum in Berlin.

These sphinxes, again carved from the great blocks at the sides of the doorway, approach sculpture in the round. Large **wings** are portrayed at their sides and over the two freestanding hind legs rises the **tail** of a cat, curling into a spiral above. The feminine faces with inset eyes were framed by **thick twists of hair**, which fall in full locks onto the chest. The creatures wear **helmets** with short cheek guards. **Horns** at the front of the helmets signify their divinity. The standard-like boughs of six rosettes on the helmets have been restored in analogy with the surviving sphinx at the exterior doorway. The sphinxes of the gate at Nişantaş (Figs. 113-114) also boasted such ornament, as can be seen on the example in the Boğazkale Museum garden.

The function of the Sphinx Gate. The Sphinx Gate was certainly no ordinary gate, for from the outside it could be approached only by the two steep and narrow staircases at either end of the rampart. The open entrance on the city-side, flanked by the elaborate pair of sphinxes sculpted nearly in the round, brings to mind the entrance of a shrine. One could easily imagine that the exterior door would have been opened only on special occasions; the rampart of Yerkapı might then have served as a gigantic stage. The audience would have stood below in anticipation, perhaps, of priests emerging from the doorway with the cult statue of the god. Wide speculation is possible here.

Fig. 74 The sphinx from the west of the inner doorway

Fig. 75 The sphinx from the east of the inner doorway

The Temple District in the Upper City

(General Plan: No.19)

From the top of the rampart at Yerkapı (nearly 1,250 m above sea level) you have a marvellous view out over the valley – some 300 m below – that stretches a good ten kilometers off to the north/northwest (Fig. 76). This fertile strip was once filled with the farmsteads of those raising food for the Hittite capital; in times of danger the families living here could take refuge within the city walls.

The outlines of nearly all the foundations you see in the hollow below Yerkapı represent **Hittite temples** (Figs. 77-82). By the period of the Hittite Empire once the great city wall had been erected in the south for protection, this area had grown into a well established **cult center**. So far, in addition to Temples 2 and 3

Fig. 76 The view northwards from Yerkapı. The green band in the background traces the course of the Budaközü stream across the plain

(General Plan: Nos. 21 and 20), which lie above the central temple district on the prominent spur to the SE – on your right – 24 different temples have been identified here (Fig. 82). Still other sacred buildings include Temple 5, which stands further to the east near the King's Gate (General Plan: No. 22); Temple 30, which lies further off to the west near the Lion Gate (General Plan: No. 14); and Temple 7 on the saddle behind Sarıkale (General Plan: No. 26). We may assume that still more temples lay in the central cult center here; not without reason the Hittite texts frequently mention "**the Thousand Gods of the Hatti-Land**". The phrase expresses Hittite tradition quite appropriately; the deities of other cities and peoples were also incorporated into the cult center of Hattusha. If no temple was erected, at least a sacred stone, a sacral tree or grove, or a fountain was consecrated to the honor of the deity. Such hallowed features are frequently mentioned in the Hittite texts.

Fig. 77 Aerial view of the central Temple District in the Upper City

Fig. 78 Temples 20-22 and 24 at the east of the Temple District

Fig. 79 Temples and a Byzantine church at the north edge of the Temple District

Fig. 80 Temple 2

Fig. 81 Temple 3

79

The **dimensions of the temples** vary greatly. The larger temples range from 1,200 to 1,500 m², while the smaller ones vary from 400 to 600 m². Certain temples (Nos. 4, 6 and 26) were also surrounded by a walled-off precinct known as a *temenos*. The size of the temples and the great number of rooms indicate that the temples also served economic purposes, owning land and run by personnel responsible for the preparation and storage of raw materials and foodstuffs. Some temples may even have served an ambassadorial function for the land and people whose deity or deities they represented.

Although each temple displayed a different number and arrangement of rooms, all shared **an essential common plan** similar to that of the Great Temple in the Lower City: an entrance portal led into an open courtyard, from which one passed through an open stoa or portico into one or more antechambers leading into the adyton, or Holy of Holies, where the cult statue of the deity stood. The cult chambers can be identified by their size, as well as by the statue bases found inside. It is of note that no special direction of the compass seems to have been preferred, either for the orientation of the temples or for that of the cult chambers themselves.

The **construction method and materials** reflect those employed in Hattusha in general. What remains today are the foundations and parts of the wall socle, built of limestone blocks. The walls of timber frame construction filled with mudbrick, and the flat roofs of timbers plastered with mud are, of course, no longer in place. The walls would have been plastered over and the interiors – at least partially – decoratively painted. We assume that the temples were generally only one story high, although those built on the slope often featured a cellar. While the more recent temples

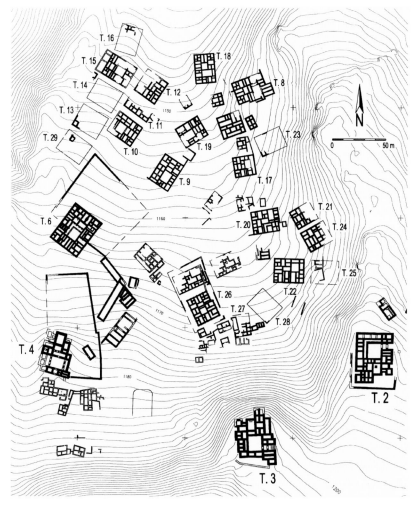

Fig. 82 Plan of the central Temple District with temples numbered from 2 through 29 (with 5 and 7 elsewhere)

demonstrate a consistently rectangular plan, three of the older structures featured a configuration with projections. These latter are Temples 2 and 3 high on the spurs to the southeast, and Temple 4, which sits on a small rise in the west of the hollow.

Fig. 83-85 Hittite masons spared no efforts to fit the stone blocks perfectly. Striking parallels can be seen in Inca masonry

Unfortunately no clues remain to identify the deities worshipped in these temples. The cult statues of metal or wood (often covered with sheets of metal foil) have long since disappeared, and little else was left in the chambers, as most of the temples had gone out of use and been completely cleared out before the fall of the city. Among the dedicatory offerings in the temples there certainly would have been ceramic vessels and bronze weapons.

Fig. 86 A block with numerous dowel holes

Fig. 87 The pierced cover stone of a drain in the court of Temple 2

Toward the end of the 13th century, however, **the temple district underwent a transformation.** Where earlier only temples had stood, there were now houses and workshops. By this period the might of the Hittite Empire was dwindling and external dangers were threatening. Parts of the population that had long been living outside the city gates must now have moved in to settle here in the former temple district. At the southern edge of the hollow you can see some remnants of the small and irregular structures of their abodes. The diverse foundations to the north, on the other hand, represent the remains of **Byzantine farmsteads,** and indeed there is a small church (General Plan: No. 25; Fig. 168) still standing from this later period.

Fig. 88 Temple 5 with the King's Gate in the background (top right)

Temple 5 *(General Plan: No.22)*

On your way from Yerkapı to the King's Gate you will pass the three largest temples of the Upper City. A fair proportion of the wall socles, constructed of great limestone blocks, are preserved in all three. Whereas Temples 2 (Fig. 80) and 3 (Fig. 81) still form a part of the temple district, you encounter Temple 5 lying further down near the King's Gate, at the eastern side of the great southern bow of the city wall (Fig. 88-91). Due to the massive masonry and orthostates employed in the structure, the excavators first interpreted it as a palace. The **temple plan** eventually became apparent in this structure as well, however. One entered the building through a gateway at the end of a long ramp; here was an open court and opposite, the entrance of a portico, behind which two small rooms led into the cult chamber itself,

Fig. 89 Looking southwestward from Temple 5 towards the rampart at Yerkapı

distinguished by its dimensions as well as by a base for the cult statue. On the plan it is clear, however, that the identical architectural sequence was repeated if someone standing in the courtyard turned 90° to his left: again he would see the colonnaded stoa, antechamber and large cult chamber with a statue base. We recognize, therefore, that this temple – like Temple 1 – was another sanctuary dedicated to **two deities**. A further resemblance between these two temples, not to mention the size (Temple 5 is very slightly smaller in area than Temple 1), is seen in the small free-standing structure – perhaps an altar – in the right-hand corner of the inner court. A significant difference between the two temples is the arrangement of the two groups of rooms, which here both open off the west side of the building. This may reflect the different construction date of Temple 5.

Fig. 90 The court of Temple 5 (K. Krause)

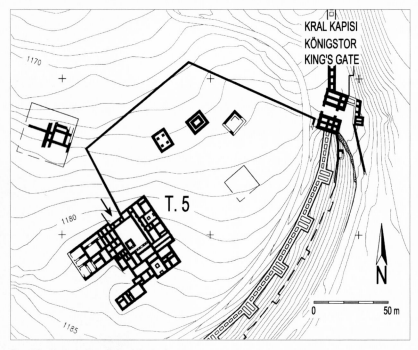

KRAL KAPISI
KÖNIGSTOR
KING'S GATE

1170

1180

T. 5

1185

0   50 m

N

Fig. 91 Temple 5 and the King's Gate

Temple 5, like some of the temples in the central temple district, was also connected to an **enclosure wall** that grouped the temple and several further structures within a temenos, or sacred precinct. Three small one-room structures might be compared to chapels; they may have been smaller additional shrines. A **stele** with the representation of a warrior in a short skirt and horned pointed hat, holding a lance, was found in one of these (Fig. 92); it is now on display in the Çorum Museum. The hieroglyphics above the raised hand of the warrior indicate that the sculpture portrays the Great King Tudhaliya. Because the horns on the headgear symbolize the power of a god, the stele apparently depicts a king already departed from this world and raised into the heavens. With three or even four of the Great Hittite Kings bearing the same name, the identification is not clear.

Fig. 92 The Great King Tudhaliya on a stele from a building near Temple 5

The King's Gate *(General Plan: No.23)*

This gate in the east of the great southern bow of the city wall corresponds to the Lion Gate in the west (Fig. 91). Here also we have two **towers flanking the gate**, which again consists of two doorways built as parabolic arches. The relief decoration on this gate, however, was not on the exterior, but faced inward toward the city (Fig. 93).

The Warrior Relief. This sculpture of a warrior in high relief – parts of it more than half in the round – measures 2.25 m from the top of the helmet to the tip of the toe (Figs. 95-96). The original, cut from its block in the doorway in 1907, can be seen today in the Museum of Ancient Civilizations in Ankara. Dressed only in a short, richly patterned **wrap-around skirt**, the warrior carries

Fig. 93 The King's Gate after excavation in 1907

Fig. 94 The exterior of the King's Gate

a **short sword** with a crescent grip tucked into his wide **belt**; the end of the sheath curls upward. In his hand he holds a decorated **axe** with the ends of its blade curving backwards and four thorny spurs at its heel. On his head he wears a pointed **helmet** with wide cheek-guards and a protective collar. His long **hair** falls to his shoulders at the back, and a **ribbon** attached to the peak of his helmet hangs to elbow-length. One curving **horn** is sculpted at the front of the helmet; the observer must picture a second out of sight at the back.

The **identity** of the warrior remains a mystery. The excavators took him for a king, and thus the gate received its name. Because horns on the helmet are attributes of the gods, our warrior is more likely to be the **representation of a god,** however. He may

Fig. 95 The god armed with axe and sword at the King's Gate

Shortly after the discovery of the warrior, the question arose as to whether 'he' might be a 'she': an Amazon. It was the configuration of the breasts and the size of the nipples that prompted certain scholars to suggest this possibility. Closer inspection, however, revealed enough hair depicted on the chest to rule out any question of the warrior being female.

Fig. 97 The city gates opened early in the morning

Fig. 98-99 The heavy wooden doors are long gone; only pivot stones and holes for the wooden bolts on the inner side of the gate remain

well be Sharrumma, son of the weather-god Teshub and the sun-goddess Hepat, patron and protector of the Great King Tudhaliya IV.

This interpretation introduces yet another aspect to the situation. This gateway might have been something other than a normal passageway, for who would portray the image of a god on a common doorpost, so to speak, subject to the touch of any and all passers-by? Might the relief represent the sanctity of an Upper City not open to everyone? Interpreting the statue as a deity also brings to mind the possibility that this gate was only opened for special cultic processions.

Fig. 100 Outer fortifications with bastion at the King's Gate

Fig. 101 Reconstruction of the King's Gate (U. Betin after P. Neve)

Construction of the Gate. In size and construction the King's Gate very closely corresponds to the Lion Gate; it is like a mirror image (Figs. 91; 93-94). The towers flanking both gates measure approximately 10 x 15 m, and the parabolic archways themselves measure 3.25 m across at the base; at both gates the arches stood about 5 m high. A **pair of wooden doors** once swung open and closed here. The stone **sockets** which held the **pivots** on which the doors swung are still visible at the corners, and on the exterior thresholds you can see **traces of scraping** left by the heavy wooden doors. As at the Lion Gate, the outer doorway could be barred from inside; in the lateral walls of the passages there are holes to receive the **bolts** (Fig. 98-99).

The **exterior of the gateway** is better preserved (and reconstructed) here, so that you have a better idea of the defense system and approach outside (Figs. 91; 100-101). The **approach ramp** led steeply upward alongside the outer fortification of the city wall. Additional fortifications across the ramp on the valley side included a bastion, so that any enemy approaching the gate could be attacked from two sides at once. The idea was to keep the enemy away from the actual entranceway as long as possible, for although the wooden doors were strong, they were still of wood and thus vulnerable to battering rams and – above all – to fire.

The Eastern Ponds *(General Plan: No.24)*

Along a hollow southeast of the Southern Citadel the Hittites fashioned two **small artificial lakes** (Fig. 102, right), the extent of which is indicated by the reinforced sloping banks which have been restored (and partially reconstructed) here (Fig. 103). **Pond 1** measures about 60x90 m. Although only the northern edges of **Pond 2**, lying behind it to the southeast, were excavated, the lay of the land here indicates that it could not have been much smaller. A **dam**, 16 m across at the base, separated the two, and similar constructions were used to reinforce the NE banks of both ponds and the NW bank of Pond 1.

The **edges of the basins** were formed by shallow sloping embankments cobbled with limestone. The embankment of Pond 1 on the slope toward the street was two meters in height; on the other sides it must have been still higher. The **bottom** of the ponds, rather than being paved, was simply plastered with a **watertight layer of clay**; the underlying rock is serpentine, which permits only minimal seepage.

Insulating the paved embankments proved much more of a challenge, and here the Hittite engineers came up with a rather ingenious solution. Deep, narrow trenches were opened behind the embankments and filled with watertight clay, thus minimizing the seepage. Even today – after some 3,250 years – the system remains effective; in the early summer, when the ground round about has completely dried out, the soil here where the ponds once were remains soft and muddy.

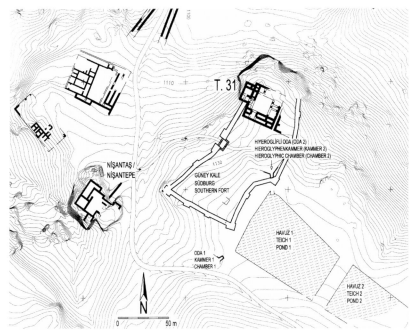

Fig. 102 Excavation in the eastern part of the upper city: the Eastern Ponds, the Southern Citadel and Nişantaş

Fig. 103 The northwestern part of Pond 1 and the fortress of the Southern Citadel

97

Fig. 104 Clay segments of a Hittite water pipeline. Stone-covered holes in each segment facilitated maintenance and repair

Several **springs** fed the ponds. One of these, above the street, still flows year round. Because still more water was necessary, however, a system of clay pipes (Fig. 104) was installed to bring in water from springs outside the city, and a pipeline passes through the city walls below the King's Gate for this purpose.

Chamber 1 *(General Plan: No.27)*

The two eastern ponds were so located that they could serve as a water reservoir for a great part of the city. Their connection with a **cult**, however, is beyond doubt, as demonstrated by two monumental domed chambers, one at the western and one at the northern corner of Pond 1. From the paved street you can spot Chamber 1, which survived in poor condition and could be only partially restored (Figs. 102; 105). You see a room some 4 m deep with a steep 3 m high dome; exterior walls taper inward towards the dome like a funnel. Chambers 1 and 2 represent **the oldest domes of stone masonry known in the Near East.**

Fig. 105 Chamber 1

The chamber was not freestanding, but built into the south-western end of an earthen dam (as is indicated by the earth heaped up over the chamber). The dam ran parallel to the embankment of Pond 1, and parts of it were later incorporated into the Iron-Age defenses of the Southern Citadel (seen behind the chamber). A second identical stone chamber (= Chamber 2, also known as the Hieroglyph Chamber) is located to the north of the pond at the opposite end of the dam. It has been possible to fully reconstruct Chamber 2, which survived with relief sculpture in excellent condition.

Fig. 106 Chamber 2; in the background, the rampart of Yerkapı

Chamber 2, The Hieroglyph Chamber
(General Plan: No.28)

When first discovered, this chamber was believed to be a tomb, which explains the frequent reference to it as a chamber tomb or a royal grave. That its role is basic to cult practice, however, has now become clear; it seems possible that the chamber represented a symbolic entrance to the Underworld (Figs. 106-107).

Not all of the limestone blocks from which the chamber had been constructed were left in place; many were found scattered throughout the general area, for they had been 'borrowed' after a few centuries and used in building the defenses of the Iron Age

Fig. 107 Chamber 2; the pointed vault was rather unstable and probably did not stand for a very long time

Fig. 108   The Sun God in relief on the back wall of Chamber 2

fortress just above, known as the Southern Citadel. The reconstruction of the chamber was therefore like a giant three-dimensional jigsaw puzzle, for each block was individually cut and 'tailored' to its position; no two blocks were the same. In the end there were only a very few blocks missing, and these pieces were then cut from a yellowish sandstone. The massive exterior walls that close in over the chamber, on the other hand, have been completely rebuilt – on the original foundations, of course, and with the reuse of old stone blocks.

The chamber was adorned with **reliefs** that have survived in excellent condition thanks to the blanket of earth under which they lay protected over

Fig. 109 The Great King Shupiluliuma II on the left wall of Chamber 2; he is portrayed as a warrior with bow, sword and lance

the millennia. On the back wall stands a **sun- god** in a long cloak and slippers curling up at the toe (Fig. 108). Identified by the double winged sun positioned over his head, he holds a curved

Fig. 110 Luvian hieroglyphic inscription commissioned by the Great King Shupuluiliurna II on the right-hand wall of Chamber 2

Fig. 111 The inscription of Chamber 2

rod in his left hand, and in his right – as befits a giver of life – a somewhat modified version of **the Egyptian ankh – the emblem of life.** The representation – like that of the warrior on the wall to the left – is executed in remarkably low relief without any indication of detail. Further configuration has perhaps been left to the painter.

The relief to the left represents Shupiluliuma II, the last of the famous Great Kings of Hattusha and the ruler responsible for the construction of the chamber. He is portrayed in the short skirt of the **warrior,** a sword in his belt and a lance in his right hand; a bow is slung over his shoulder (Fig. 109). On his feet you can make out slippers curling up at the toes, and on his head he wears the pointed hat typical of divinities; this one has three horns at the front. Before him are his title and name, inscribed in Luvian hieroglyphics. The Great King apparently had himself portrayed as a god even though he was still alive and active at the time, as is confirmed on the wall opposite.

We have **a six-line inscription in Luvian hieroglyphics** chiseled into the wall opposite (Figs. 110-111). (Luvian hieroglyphics are a picture-script developed in Anatolia; neither linguistically nor pictorially do they have anything to do with Egyptian hieroglyphics). The inscription begins at the upper right. Upon closer inspection and a comparison of the symbols, you will see that some of the signs appear like mirror-writing. This is because the inscription was written continuously across one line and back the next – first right to left then left to right, a technique known as *boustrophedon:* "as the ox plows".

Although the inscription has yet to be completely deciphered, the main gist of it is clear: the Great King Shupiluliuma reports that with the blessings of the gods he has conquered several lands, including that of Tarhuntasha, and that he has founded new cities and made sacrifices to the gods at various locations. The last sentence mentions "a divine earth-road". D. Hawkins, a specialist on Luvian hieroglyphs, accepts this as the **dedicatory building inscription** stating the purpose of the structure, here indicated as a passage leading into the earth, into the underground. The ponds behind the chamber now take on a further significance, for in the mind of antiquity lakes and springs represented passages to the Underworld. If Hawkins' interpretation is correct, the chamber might have been a **symbolic entrance to the Underworld**, and therefore would have played a significant role in cult practice. Although there is no similar inscription in Chamber 1, the two chambers were built together and in the same relationship to the ponds; they must certainly be considered as a single entity.

The Southern Citadel and Temple 31

(General Plan: Nos. 29 and 30)

One of the few standing monuments in Hattusha that do not stem from Hittite times is the "Phrygian" Southern Citadel, built shortly **after 700 BC** (Figs. 102-103; 112). It was part of a fairly large Iron Age settlement that spread far into certain areas of the Lower City as well as occupying the eastern reaches of the Upper City. There was also a large Iron Age citadel built upon the site of the Hittite Royal Citadel at Büyükkale, i.e. the plateau situated about 100 m to the north of the Southern Citadel.

Fig. 112   The Southern Citadel, a fortress built towards the middle of the Iron Age (7th-6th centuries BC); in the background, the Royal Citadel of the Hittites at Büyükkale

The **Iron Age fortification walls** were built on a massive socle of quarrystone; here at the Southern Citadel these foundations were some four meters across. Upon this there must have been a mudbrick superstructure similar to that of the Hittites, with a mudbrick and timber construction corporating towers and battlements. A single **gate** flanked by towers led into the complex from the northwest. Inside were **residences, workshops and storehouses**. Along your way upwards from the gate to the Hieroglyphic Chamber you see the restoration of various

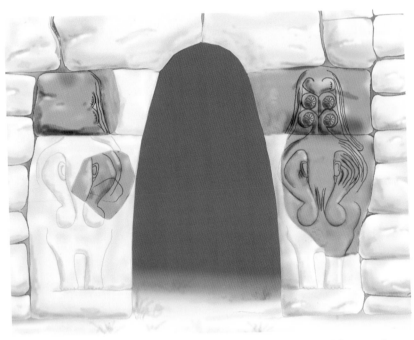

Fig. 113 Reconstruction of the Sphinx Gate at the entrance to the building complex on Nişantaş; darker shaded parts indicate what is preserved of the original (U. Betin after P. Neve)

foundations from the Iron Age. These structures, too, were built with walls of mudbrick and most probably had flat roofs like those of the Hittite buildings.

In the northern half of the Southern Citadel (to the left on your way towards the Hieroglyphic Chamber) the remains of a large Hittite structure known as **Temple 31** have been excavated. On the plan the large interior courtyard characteristic of the temple layout is immediately apparent (Fig. 102). This temple may have been contingent to the cult practices involved with Chambers 1 and 2 and the ponds.

Fig. 114   The right-hand sphinx from the gate at Nişantaş

Nişantaş/Nişantepe *(General Plan: No.31)*

This is – in addition to Sarıkale and Yenicekale – still another rock outcropping in the Upper City of Hattusha. A **grand edifice** once stood on top of the cliffs here (Fig. 102); rock cuttings and the occasional block still in place reveal the original outline of the walls. Blocks from a **gate** were recovered among the fallen debris at the base of the cliff face. It had been fitted out with the fore-parts of two great **Sphinxes**, very much like those on the exterior of the Sphinx Gate at Yerkapı (Figs. 113-114). On the remaining fragments of the sphinxes (now in the Boğazkale Museum garden) you can still make out the impressive hood-like manes or hairdos, locks of which fall onto the breast, and the high standard-like bough of 6 rosettes atop the headdress. The entrance of this gateway, also parabolic in form, originally stood

Fig. 115 Inscription in Luvian hieroglyphs at Nişantaş

at the top of an entrance **ramp** leading into the building complex that once stood on the cliffs here. Unfortunately – as is the case with the constructions on the other rock pinnacles as well – we are left with little idea as to the original function.

The Inscription. The name of the site is identified by a large inscription in **Luvian hieroglyphics** on the side of the cliff (Nişantaş = marked rock). The 8.5-m long inscription, eleven lines in length, was chiseled onto a smoothed surface on the cliff face (Figs. 115-116). The hieroglyphic signs once resembled those in Chamber 2, but have become badly weathered through exposure to the elements; as a result much of the **content of the text** has never been deciphered. It is clear that it stems from the rule of Shupiluliuma II, the last of the well known Great Kings of Hattusha. In the top line (that is fairly legible on a clear day at

Fig. 116 Detail of the inscription

around one o'clock in the afternoon) you can see his name, written from right to left, followed by that of his father Tudhaliya IV and his grandfather Hatushili III. Then comes another mention of Tudhaliya. We surmise that the Great King mentions the construction of a monument for his father (= perhaps Chamber B of the rock-cut sanctuary of Yazılıkaya) here, as well as reporting some of his other accomplishments, including a battle at sea followed by a landing on Cyprus. Known to the Hittites as Alashiya, the island of Cyprus – due to its rich sources of copper – was the object of much strife in antiquity.

In the area **north of Nişantaş**, which lay directly before the Royal Citadel of Büyükkale, stood several **official buildings**. Just west of the paved road you see the reconstructed foundations of the "North Complex" (Fig. 117; General Plan: No. 32); behind it on the slope stood the "West Building", only a few basement walls of which survived. In these cellar rooms, however, more than three thousand clay nodules came to light; these were the *bullae* that carried the seal impressions of the Great Kings and their officials. A clay *bulla* served the function of a lead seal; it distinguished written correspondence and various goods as "official business". Objects were tied up with string or leather strips that were then sealed by pressing a bit of clay around them; upon this piece of clay, or *bulla*, an insignia from an official stone or metal seal would be impressed (Fig. 118). An intense fire which broke out in this building then destroyed everything but the *bullae*, which were baked – like clay in a kiln – and preserved for posterity.

Fig. 117 Foundations of the "North Complex" at Nişantaş

Fig. 118
Seal impression of
the Great King
Tudhaliya IV on a
clay bulla

113

Fig. 119
The Royal
Citadel of
Büyükkale
from the air

Fig. 120 Büyükkale from the southwest

The Royal Citadel of Büyükkale

(General Plan: No.33)

Büyükkale (= Great Fortress) is indeed an ideal place to establish a **royal residence**. This plateau with a relatively flat surface about 250x140 m is naturally protected on every side by steep slopes or precipitous bluffs (Figs. 119-122). It was inhabited as early as the 3rd millennium BC by people of the Early Bronze Age; the Hittites then developed it little by little into a well fortified citadel. Still later it was put to good advantage by the "Phrygians" of the Iron Age and by settlers of the Hellenistic period.

The architectural remains visible on Büyükkale today present a general impression of how the complex must have looked after the great period of restoration and renovation carried out in the 13th century BC.

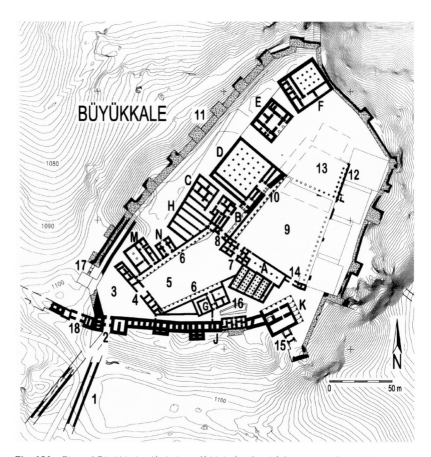

Fig. 121 Plan of Büyükkale: 1) viaduct, 2) Main (or South) Gate to the Royal Citadel,
3) the Court of the Citadel Gate, 4) entrance to the Lower Court,
5) the Lower Court, 6) stoas, 7) gateway to the Central Court, 8) side gate,
9) Central Court, 10) entrance to the reception hall in building D,
11) northwestern fortification wall, 12) ridge (artificial platform) with silo pits
(or cisterns?) 13) the Upper Court, 14) small gate to the Upper Court, 15) the
East Gate, 16) pool, 17) the Southwest Gate, and 18) the gate in the Postern
Wall. See text for descriptions of buildings A-N.

Circular Tour (the numbers refer to the plan Fig. 121). The staircase by which you reach the Royal Citadel is modern; originally a great **viaduct (1)** led upwards from the south to the citadel gate. A reconstruction of the side walls of this viaduct are to be seen just east of the paved street at the foot of the stairs (and to the west of the street you can see remnants of a still older viaduct). These stone walls served as a substructure for a high mud-brick construction across which the roadway would have passed. The flooring may have been of wooden beams, something suitable for horse-drawn vehicles.

Only the right-hand (= eastern) side of the Main Gate to the Royal Citadel, the **South Gate (2)** is still standing. It was again a gate with two doorways (Fig. 123); flanking the outer door stood two lions similar to those at the Lion Gate. Passing through, you enter what is known as the **Court of the Citadel Gate (3)**. Here a **pavement of flat red stones** originally conducted the visitor across the center of the court to a **gate (4)** opening into the Lower Court of the Citadel. A comparison with the "red-carpet reception" received by dignitaries today is indeed appropriate here.

The relatively long and drawn out **Lower Court of the Citadel (5)** is the second in a series of four courtyards varying in size. As you can see on the plan, this court was bordered by long **colonnaded porches,** or **stoas (6)**. (The plan shows many details not visible *in situ* today, for certain features have been re-covered with a protective layer of earth.) We assume that the various structures surrounding this court (Fig. 124), Buildings M, N, H, G and A, served as **residences** of the **palace officials** as well as shelter for the "Bearers of the Golden Lances", that is to say, the **palace**

Fig. 122 Reconstruction of the palace complex on Büyükkale (U. Betin after P. Neve)

Fig. 123 Reconstruction of the viaduct and the South Gate to Büyükkale (P. Neve)

Fig. 124 Büyükkale. View across the Lower Court

guard. At the opposite end of the Lower Court stood an imposing **gateway** (7) providing admittance to the Central Court. This structure, the walls of which still stand to an impressive height, originally featured a staircase and was flanked by two lions "standing guard". It thus provided an optical as well as a physical barrier between the outer courts and the palace area proper. The **Central Court of the Citadel (9)** that lay behind this gateway was also surrounded by colonnades.

Today's pathway, however, takes you along the left side of the Lower Court past Buildings M, N and H. From here you pass through a second **gate** (8) into the **nucleus of the palace**. Behind the gate to the right you can see a **drain** which carried off both rainwater and palace sewage. To your left stood **Buildings B and**

Fig. 125 Reconstruction of Building C (U. Betin after P. Neve)

C, interpreted as **internal shrines** somewhat comparable to the chapel of the European castle. In the middle of Building C was a **pool** 5.2x6 meters and at least 2.3 m deep; in it were found a variety of ceramic vessels, apparently votive offerings. The walls were built of unusually large limestone blocks, and a drainage channel led out through the northern corner. The room may have been an atrium, roofed only around the sides with the pool open to the sky (Fig. 125).

Adjoining this complex was the largest structure on Büyükkale, **Building D**, the upper floor of which is thought to have served as the King's **reception hall** (9). What you see today is only the lower story, 39x48 m, with five long division walls. These served as a foundation for five rows of pillars in the upper story, where there

Fig. 126 Reconstruction of the reception or audience hall in Building D
(U. Betin after R. Naumann)

Fig. 127 Reconstruction of Building E (U. Betin after R. Naumann)

would have been a square hall 32 m on a side, its ceiling supported by wooden pillars (Fig. 126). This hall would have had a
direct entrance through a **portal** (10) opening off the Central
Court.

Fig. 128   Burnt mudbrick walls of Building E (now encased by protective masonry)

At the end of this series of buildings along the northwest side of Büyükkale, then, stood **Building E** and **Building F**, which must have comprised the **private apartments of the King**. From here, in privacy at the far back – in the innermost reaches of the Citadel – one has a fantastic view out over the city and across the valley receding into the north. The landscape in the gorge below is fascinating as well. With a little luck, gazing downward (!) you may glimpse a vulture – or even an eagle – soaring by. As early as 1906 an extensive **archive of clay tablets** was excavated in Building E (Fig. 127) and on the slope before it.

The great **conflagration** that destroyed the palace complexes at the end of the 13th century BC fired part of the clay walls of the buildings like pottery in a kiln. Those here in building E were by chance exceptionally well preserved (Fig. 128). Their remains are

Fig. 129 The eastern side of Büyükkale; Hittite fortification walls are visible on the Eastern Plateau just to the left of center of the photograph

today encased by a protective outer masonry that protects the originals from weathering; thus the plump, rounded remnants you see today in no way reflect the original appearance of the walls here.

An impressive **fortification wall (11)** at the northwest separates the Royal Citadel from the city below. It continued still further around the very steep slope to the east above the deep valley (Fig. 129); here you can still make out many scattered remnants of the masonry, although in places only the beddings cut in the rock to receive the great stone blocks remain. Holes in the rock testify that **dowels** were used to hold many of the blocks in place.

The surface in this area to the north and east is formed entirely of the exposed bedrock. Toward the southeast an **artificial set (12)** as high as 2.2 m and 24.5 m long was cut into the rise beside the

Fig. 130 Platform along the Upper Court of Büyükkale; on the horizon, the rampart of Yerkapı

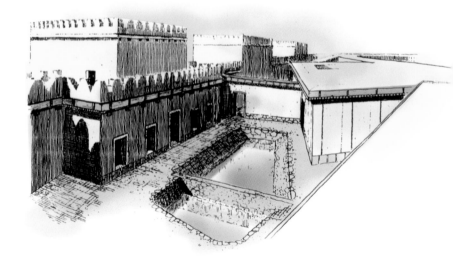

Fig. 131 Büyükkale. Reconstruction of the pool and structures G and J as seen from the northeast (P. Neve revised by U.Betin)

Fig. 132   Büyükkale. The pool (right) and Buildings G (left) and A (background)

The archives of clay tablets found in Buildings A, E
and K have played a most important role in our
research of Hittite history. The hundreds of tablets
that had been stored on wooden shelves here have
perpetuated not only contracts and official documents, but oracular prophecies, instruction in cult
practice, folklore, collections of legal decisions
and historical texts as well. While most of these
survived the burning of the palace complex, the
information included in the archives of wooden
tablets has been lost forever.

Upper Court of the Royal Citadel (13) (Fig. 130). Square depressions at regular intervals in the ground below the set indicate the **position of a row of pillars** that once formed a colonnade here. Into the set above, two **pits, probably grain silos (or cisterns)** were sunk deep into the rock. There must have been other structures standing on the platform, but these can be only hypothetically reconstructed.

The path returns from the summit of the citadel along the east side of the **Central Court (9)**. Most of the Hittite remains here still lie buried under the ruins of the 7th- and 6th-century BC "Phrygian" constructions (cf. Fig. 166). You leave the court at the former location of a small **gate (14)** which had been built here into the southwest of the court wall. From here a path once led downhill to a second citadel gate, the **East Gate (15)** on the slope below Büyükkale. (This area has been greatly disturbed by erosion.)

Between **Building K** and **Building A**, both of which contained extensive **archives of clay tablets**, you reach a small open area (Figs. 131-132) which was nearly entirely occupied by a 24-m

Fig. 133 The gate in the Postern Wall at the southwest of Büyükkale

long **pool of water** (16). Sloping embankments paved with limestone outlined this pool, which must have had some significance in cult ritual, for a quantity of small clay votive vessels were recovered from the mud at the bottom of the pool. It may well have had a practical function as well; it would have represented, for instance, an emergency water supply to extinguish fires which might have broken out in the citadel.

Your tour of the Royal Citadel has thus come to an end. You may be puzzled, however, that both the citadel gates you have seen were located to the south, away from the city itself. There was indeed probably a small third gate, the **Southwest Gate** (17) which lay to the west at the base of the citadel; from here one could climb up a path past Buildings M, N, and H, then proceeding alongside Building C. Opening directly into the Lower City, this gate must have been used to take provisions up to the citadel. It seems highly unlikely that it was reserved only for deliveries, however, for it represented a direct route for the King and his court to reach the Lower City. Its position here was probably also selected because of a **spring** that surfaced just here at the base of the hill; this was the shortest way to carry up drinking water, a necessity, for there was no other source on Büyükkale. Access to the spring was reorganized in the "Phrygian" Iron Age. A long staircase to the new citadel above was constructed, and in the process both the Hittite gate and the earlier passage up the hill were either disguised or destroyed.

The **Gate in the Postern Wall** (18), which you see at the foot of Büyükkale (Fig. 133) deserves mention here as well, for it represented the southern doorway of the Old City of Hattusha.

Fig. 134 The gorge of the Büyükkaya stream. Büyükkaya on the left, Ambarlıkaya on the right, and Büyükkale in the background

The Gorge and the Bridge *(General Plan: No.35)*

The valley of the Büyükkaya stream, which runs through a deep gorge just east of the Royal Citadel of Büyükkale, also cuts through the northern part of the lower city (Fig. 134). As a security measure the Hittites also incorporated the ridge of Büyükkaya across the stream into their defense system. The city wall ran northwards down the slope from the Royal Citadel into the great ravine, where it crossed the stream at its narrowest point, near the cliff called **Ambarlıkaya**, and then climbed the rocky slope up to the top of Büyükkaya. The cuttings where the huge stone blocks had been imbedded in the rock are still in evidence here, and dowel-holes as well. R. Naumann had postulated a **Hittite bridge** here, which would have crossed the streamed at a height of

15 m, before P. Neve pointed out that the steps cut on either side of the gorge here can be dated by their chisel marks to Byzantine times. In Hittite times there were probably only **defense bastions** on either side of the stream. Between these, however, it would have been possible to extend a makeshift bridge (perhaps a type of suspension bridge?) for expediency; it would not have borne much traffic, but watchmen could then have crossed freely to the other bank. Much more important was to block an enemy's possible entry into the city through the streambed. A permanent construction would have been out of the question due to the high waters in springtime. Under careful guard, a system of stable latticework could have been employed.

Büyükkaya *(General Plan: No.37)*

Seen from the Lower City, the rugged cliffs of Büyükkaya (= Great Rock) are most impressive, rising precipitously some 100 m from the valley floor (cf. Fig. 32). A small settlement existed high up on the summit about 3000 years before the arrival of the Hittites. The Early Bronze Age Hatti lived there as well, and in their turn the Hittites erected a monumental structure on the summit of Büyükkaya, of which only foundation segments survive.

The true character of Büyükkaya is visible only from "the back"; approaching from Yozgat – or on your way to Yazılıkaya and back – you notice that the rise is actually a **long high ridge** enclosed by a **fortification wall** (Fig. 135).

Originally, which is to say sometime in the 16th century BC, the fortifications ran only along the southeast, starting from the crossing in the gorge at Ambarlıkaya. They were then continued

Fig. 135 Büyükkaya from the north

to the north, over the high ridge of Büyükkaya and down, where they met the **Northern City Wall** (General Plan: No. 38), which arched in a wide bow to rejoin the Lower City and the Postern Wall. Later another fortification wall was erected on the north side of Büyükkaya, which met the *"Abschnittsmauer"* (i.e. the fortress wall cutting through the Lower City) at the rock called **Mihraplıkaya** (General Plan: No. 36). Thus the rise was transformed into an exceptionally well protected fortress. Looking up from the valley you can see the construction of the fortifications particularly well, for the foundations of the casemate wall and towers climb diagonally up the slope.

From the 16th century BC onwards, Büyükkaya was used as a giant **granary**. The supplies for the city and country were stored here in rectangular cellars dug into the earth; the floors were paved (Fig. 136). The largest of these storage bins, 11 of which have been so far discovered (there were doubtless more), measures 12x18 m and was more than 2 m deep. This alone would indicate a capacity for at least 260 tons of grain.

The granaries on Büyükkaya are not accessible, since they were filled in after excavation – to preserve the evidence, so to speak.

Fig. 136   Paved floors of the granaries on Büyükkaya

Once these bins were filled with grain, they were decked with a thick layer of soil. Thus sealed from the air, the grain used up what remained of the oxygen and gave off carbon dioxide. The resulting atmosphere deterred any damage from pests; neither vermin – rats, mice and beetles – nor fungi could survive. It was ideal preservation, and could keep the grain for years at a time. This same principle of storage is used today in many countries of the third world; indeed it is still practiced in some parts of Turkey.

Fig. 137
Reconstruction
of the granaries on
Büyükkaya (U. Betin)

The Hitite Rock Sanctuary
of Yazılıkaya

The story of the discovery of Yazılıkaya also begins in 1834 with Charles Texier, the first European traveler to visit Hattusha (Fig. 138). It did not take long, then, for the relief sculpture to inspire the fantasies of many scholars. Various travelers of the 19th century brought their sketchbooks — and some even their spades; small excavations took place. The new medium of photography reached the site early on; by 1861 Jules Delbet photographed some of the reliefs. No one, however, knew quite what to make of these many sculpted figures; the Hittites were practically unknown at the time. The reliefs, which obviously portrayed two groups encountering one another, were variously interpreted: meetings of the Amazons and the Paphlagonians, of the Medes and the Lydians, or of Heracles and Astarte with their followers. It was only much later that it was understood that the figures here represent divinities of the 13th century BC.

The **rock sanctuary of Yazılıkaya** lies about 1.5 km to the northeast of the Great Temple of the Lower City. From the village of Boğazkale you take the road leading east towards Yozgat. Yazılıkaya (= rock with writing) lies nestled between rock outcroppings at the foot of the high ridge east of Hattusha (a sign marks the turn-off). In contrast to the temples within the city, the two rooms of this sanctuary (Chambers A and B), hemmed in by natural rock faces up to 12 m high, lie open to the skies. Although the site has been in use since the 15th century BC at least, not until the 13th century did the long procession of gods and goddesses take their place here, chiseled onto the rock faces by Hittite sculptors. Researchers have conjectured that this place may be a huwaši-sanctuary or the **"House of the New Year's Celebration"**, a House of the Weather God where festivities were held to honor all the pantheon at the coming of the New Year and the beginning of spring.

Tour of the Site. The actual rock sanctuary was screened off from the outside world by a rather impressive **architectural complex**. Although only the wall socle zone remains in place, the reconstruction drawing gives an idea of how the buildings must have looked with the typical mudbrick and timber frame wall construction that was employed here as well (Fig. 139). The entrance was through a **gateway with stairs** (see Plan Fig. 140). Another flight of steps took one into **an open court,** bordered by various small chambers. Apparently this area was used for ablutions and preliminary rites; this is suggested by an altar in the courtyard. Through still another gate with steps (just about where the tall trees now stand) one would then have entered the large Chamber A.

Fig. 139 Yazılıkaya. Reconstruction of the buildings in front of the rock sanctuary (U. Betin after R. Naumann)

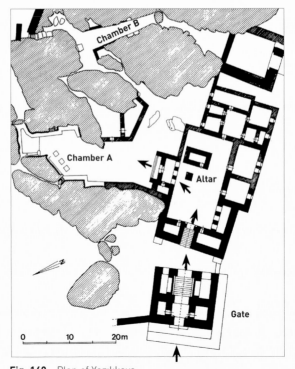

Fig. 140 Plan of Yazılıkaya

Fig. 141   Chamber A at Yazılıkaya

The light cast on the reliefs varies greatly according to the season and the time of day. In the large Chamber A, the male deities on the left can be best seen in the late morning, while the goddesses on the right show up better in the early afternoon, and the climactic scene on the back wall is best lit in the course of the afternoon (2-4 p.m.) The best light in the small Chamber B comes between 11 a.m. and 1 p.m. The reliefs were originally much easier to see. The rock when newly carved has a smooth, almost white surface (some impression of which you may get from the much better preserved reliefs in the smaller Chamber B). Furthermore, although no trace of color remains today, we assume that these reliefs were once brightly painted; nearly all early cultures were fond of bright color in their artwork and cult paintings.

Chamber A

The larger Chamber A is about 30 m long, and originally had paving on the floor (Figs. 141-142). On either side you see the **reliefs**, chiseled into panels running horizontally across the natural limestone walls. (Figs. 142 and 147 present the numbering scheme used to identify the individual reliefs). On the **left side** we have **male deities** (with the exception of relief Nos. 36 and 37); **on the right, female.** They all face the opposite end of the chamber,

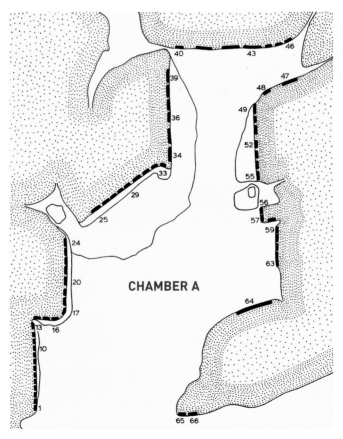

Fig. 142 Numbering system for the reliefs of Chamber A at Yazılıkaya

Fig. 143 Yazılıkaya. Relief figures (nos. 25-29) in Chamber A

towards which they appear to be slowly progressing; and there, indeed, is the **climactic tableau**: as leaders of the holy procession, the two supreme divinities, the weather god and the sun goddess greet one another.

Nearly all of the gods along the left side of the chamber (Fig. 143-144) are dressed in **short skirts** and high **pointed hats**. They all wear **shoes curling up at the toe**, and many are armed with either a sickle-shaped sword or a mace, which they carry over their shoulder. The **mountain gods** are characterized by long **"frilled"** skirts (relief Nos. 13-15, 16a and 17). Several of the gods have square-trimmed **beards**, and you can pinpoint earrings in some of their ears. Three gods are portrayed with **wings**: god Pirinkir (relief No. 31), a **moon god** (relief No. 35) and the divine **Shaushka** (relief No. 38). Behind the moon god follows the **"Sun-god of the Heavens"** (relief No. 34) identified by a winged

Fig. 144 Yazılıkaya. The line of male deities (relief nos. 1-39) in Chamber A

sun over his head. Conspicuous are two **bull-men** (relief Nos. 28 and 29; Fig. 143); they stand on the symbol for "earth" and support a crescent moon – the symbol for "the heavens" – over their heads. The only female divinities on the left are **Ninatta** and **Kulitta** (relief Nos. 36 and 37), handmaidens of the god Shaushka; they take their place behind him in the procession.

The **female divinities** on the right-hand side of the chamber (Fig. 145) are dressed in long **pleated skirts** and all wear **curling-toed shoes, earrings** and **high headdresses**. They display scarcely

any individual attributes and their entire bodies are rigidly portrayed in side profile, marching straight ahead, whereas the torsos of the males – in contrast – are rendered in front view, that is, turned toward the observer. These sex-discriminate stances are characteristic of Hittite relief sculpture in general.

The **climactic scene on the wall at the end of the chamber** (Fig. 146) portrays a meeting of the two supreme divinities, the **weather god Teshub** (relief No. 42) and the **sun goddess Hebat** (relief No. 43). The bearded god stands on the shoulders of two

Fig. 145 Yazılıkaya. The line of female deities (relief nos. 49-60) in Chamber A

mountain gods and carries a large mace. At some distance behind him appear two figures standing on mountain peaks, one probably the weather god of Hatti (relief No. 41) and one probably to be identified as **Kumarbi** (relief No. 40). The sun goddess also wears a pleated skirt and high headdress. She stands on the back of a **wild cat** that stands in turn on a series of four mountain peaks. Behind her – half hidden by her skirt – is a **prancing bull** wearing the high pointed hat of the gods; its counterpart can be seen behind the skirt of Teshub. Behind Hebat comes **Sharumma**, son of the divine pair, again placed on the back of a wild feline standing on mountain peaks. Two female figures follow him: his sister Alanzu and another girl, a granddaughter of Teshub. These two stand together over a **double-headed eagle**.

Many figures in the procession are identified by inscriptions in **Luvian hieroglypics** in front of their faces or over their outstretched arms. On top stands the symbol for "god", a horizontally placed oval with a vertical stroke down the middle. Many of the names have not yet been deciphered, and some controversy has arisen over the interpretation of others. It is interesting to note that with all deities their Hurrian name in written. The Hurrian culture of eastern Anatolia and northern Mesopotamia held a strong influence over the Hittites during the 13th and 14th centuries BC; several queens were of Hurrian background.

Fig. 146 Yazılıkaya. The climactic scene in Chamber A (relief nos. 41-46)

Under the reliefs low **bench- and pedestal-like projections** which might have been used to display offerings and decor were left protruding from the rock face at various intervals (Figs. 143-145). The long stone ledge at the left (below figures Nos. 25 through 33) displays three large rectangular depressions at the outer edge; these may have held cult accessories, incense burners for example.

1   2   3   4   5   6   7   8   9   10

16a   17   18   19

25   26   27   28   29

Fig. 147 Drawing of the reliefs of Chamber A at Yazılıkaya

34   35

40   41

36 37   38   39

42   43   44   45   46

Fig. 147 Drawing of the reliefs of Chamber A at Yazılıkaya (cont.)

46a   47   48   49   50   51

58   59   60   61   62   63

Fig. 147 Drawing of the reliefs of Chamber A at Yazılıkaya (cont.)

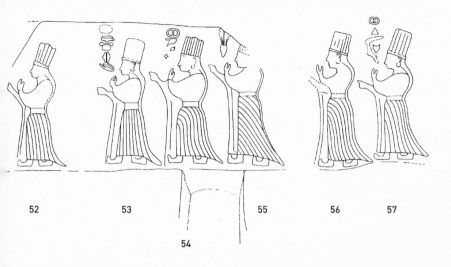

52   53   55   56   57

54

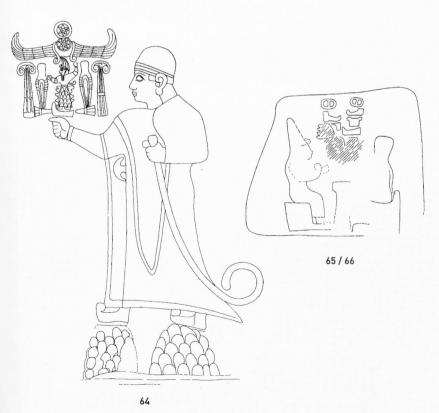

65 / 66

64

The order of the gods along the left side of Chamber A

(numbering scheme as in Figs.142 and 147)

1-12 Twelve gods of the Underworld. Twelve nearly identical male figures in short skirts and high pointed hats with a horn at the front. In their right hands they hold a sickle-shaped sword which they rest on their shoulders with the blade pointing backwards. This same row of twelve appears in Chamber B as well, where it has survived in better condition.

13-15 Three mountain gods, bearded figures wearing the same horned hats. Their full-length skirts with frills visually symbolize mountains and springs. Names in hieroglyphics (not yet recognized) accompany Nos. 14 and 15.

16 Unidentified god. A male figure wearing a short skirt and a pointed hat. His name has not yet been deciphered.

16a-17 Two mountain gods. Bearded figures wearing frilled skirts and pointed hats bent forward. Thanks to a layer of deposit, parts of No. 16a in particular have survived in especially good condition. The names have not yet been deciphered.

18-22 Five divinities with no identification. All wear the typical short skirt and high pointed hat with horns, but Nos. 20 and 22 boast a long open cloak or shawl as well. Nos. 18 and 21 are armed with maces.

23-24 Two bearded gods in short skirts and pointed hats. Both carry maces, and No. 24 also has a cloak. Names written above their extended left arms have not yet been deciphered.

25-27 Three gods dressed in short skirts and pointed hats. All carry sickle-shaped swords over their right shoulders. No name is preserved for No. 25; No. 26 may be the god Pishaishapi, and No. 27 should be Nergal, god of the Underworld.

28-29 Two creatures with the hindquarters of a bull but with an apparently human torso and arms. You can make out their tufted tails tucked beween their hind legs. They must be the Bulls of the Heavens, Hurri and Sheri; they stand on the symbol for "earth" (a rectangle with double extensions at either end) and hold the symbol for "sky" (a reclining crescent moon) over their heads.

30 Most likely the war god ZABABA (= Heshue). A masculine figure wearing a short skirt and pointed hat and carrying a sickle-shaped sword over his right shoulder.

31 The god Pirinkir. An apparently unarmed male figure wearing a short skirt and a round cap. Wings rise steeply from his shoulders.

32 An unknown god of protection, deer god. A male figure wearing a short skirt and pointed hat with horns. He carries a sickle-shaped sword over his right shoulder.

33 The war god Ashtabi. A male figure in a short skirt and pointed hat with horns. He carries a sickle-shaped sword over his right shoulder.

34 "Sun-God of the Heavens." A male figure in a long robe and shawl. On his head is a rounded cap and in his right hand a long staff or wand (*lituus*) that spirals upward at the lower end. The crescent-shaped grip of a sword protrudes below his outstretched left arm. A star-like sun-disk between a wide outspread pair of wings floats over his head.

35 A moon god. A bearded figure in a horned pointed hat, a short skirt and a long shawl. A crescent moon sits atop his hat, and wings rise from his shoulders.

36-37 Ninatta and Kulitta, attendants of the god Shaushka (No. 38). Two female figures wearing blouses and long pleated skirts. Both have round caps; No. 36 carries what seems to be a mirror in her right hand, while No. 37 holds what is probably a vial of salve or ointment. This rather deep-set relief preserves some of the original surface.

38 Shaushka, an alternative embodiment of the goddess Ishtar. A male figure with horned pointed hat, a short skirt and an over-skirt which falls in multiple folds, as well as a cloak. Wings rise steeply from his shoulders.

39 Ea, the God of Wisdom. A bearded figure with horned pointed hat, short skirt and a long cloak. He carries a mace over his right shoulder.

The climactic scene on the end-wall of Chamber A

40   Most probably the god Kumarbi. A bearded figure with a high pointed hat, a short skirt and a cloak. Behind his wide belt you can make out the crescent handle of a sword. He stands on two high stump-like "podiums" that represent mountains.

41   Probably the weather god of Hatti. A bearded figure with a pointed hat upon which a sitting bull is portrayed. He wears a short skirt and a cloak open in the front. In his belt he carries a sword with a crescent grip, in his right hand a large mace, and in his left a long staff (a lance?). Like No. 40 he stands on two mountain peaks.

42   The weather god Teshub. A bearded figure with a short skirt and a high hat adorned with many horns. He carries a short sword with a crescent grip in his belt at his left; in his right hand he holds a mace. He stands on the shoulders of two bearded figures identified as mountain gods – probably Namni and Hazzi – by the type of hat and the frilled skirts they wear. Behind Teshub's legs can be seen a prancing bull wearing the hat of divinity; it is identified in an accompanying inscription as "the bull calf of Teshub".

The relief figures Nos 1 to 42 all face to your right. Nos. 42 and 43 represent the meeting of the two most honored deities, who take their place at the head of two contingents of male and female divinities. The figures following No. 43 thus all face to your left.

43   The sun goddess Hebat. A female figure wearing a full blouse and a long pleated skirt, belted. She wears a high headdress suggestive of battlements on a city wall. A long twist of hair falls down her back to the waist. She is poised on the back of a large wild feline, which stands in turn on four low hills. Behind her is a counterpart to the prancing bull calf behind Teshub, but the hieroglyphic identification here remains undeciphered.

44   The god Sharrumma, son of Hebat and Teshub, the only male in the procession to the right. He wears a short skirt and a pointed hat with a line of horns up the front. A long twist of hair falls down his back, and in his belt he carries a crescent-hafted sword on his right (!); in his left hand is a battle axe. He, too, stands on the back of a wild cat, the tail of which ascends almost vertically. In his right hand Sharrumma holds a leash attached to the neck of the feline, which is depicted astride two mountain peaks.

45-46   Alanzu, the daughter of Teshub and Hebat, accompanied by the granddaughter of Teshub. Two female figures in long pleated skirts and blouses not as full or flowing as that of Hebat. From under their high headdresses – resembling that worn by Hebat – a twist of long hair descends to the waist. The two stand above the image of a double-headed eagle.

The order of the goddesses along the right side of Chamber A

The goddesses in general display fewer individual characteristics than the gods opposite them. Like the females at the head of the procession, they all wear shoes curling up at the toe, full-length skirts, belts, blouses, shawls or cloaks and the high headdresses that resemble battlements. A twist of hair falls down their backs, and they stand with their right hands extended in fists and their left hands – open – raised from the elbow toward their chins. Noteworthy here as well is that all females stand with their entire bodies depicted in profile, whereas the torsos – at least the chests – of the male figures appear frontally.

46a   Possibly the goddess Tarru Takitu; only the identifying hiero-glyphs are preserved; the figure itself has been badly damaged. Inserted in the rock fissure between the main scene and this goddess (now walled up for preservation) there must have been still more figures carved on separate blocks. One block which could have originally stood here is on display in the Boğazkale Museum. It portrays the goddess Ishtar.

47   The goddess Hutena.

48   The goddess Hutellurra.

49   The goddess Allatu. The niche in the rock above the head was probably carved to hold a separate block, thus repairing a defective part of the rock.

50-51   Unknown goddesses.

52   The goddess Shalush.

53   The goddess Tapkina, wife of the God of Wisdom Ea.

54   The goddess Nikkal, wife of the moon god.

55   The goddess Aya, wife of the sun god.

56-63   Goddesses without certain identification.

Two more relief figures carved on separate blocks of stone must have stood between Nos. 55 and 56.

Fig. 148 Yazılıkaya. Relief of the Great King Tudhaliya IV (relief no.64) in Chamber A

Relief Number 64:
The Great King Tudhaliya IV.

The largest relief figure in the sanctuary stands on the wall opposite the climactic scene, at the end of the procession of goddesses (Fig. 148). Represented here, as indicated, is no god, but the Great King Tudhaliya IV, directly opposite – if at a respectful distance – the meeting of the gods, as if he was paying his respects to the highest deities. For this reason as well we assume it was this Great King who was responsible for the final arrangements of the Yazılıkaya sanctuary around the middle of the 13th century BC.

This relief, protected by nature with a natural patina – a **layer of lime deposit** – is less weathered. It lies in shadow most of the year round, but in mid-June – just at the beginning of summer – it receives some direct sunlight for a short time in the late afternoons.

The appearance of the King is almost exactly like that of the sun god as represented here (relief No. 34) and in the Hieroglyph Chamber of the Upper City (see Fig. 108); he wears a long robe and a cloak, shoes curling at the toe, and a rounded cap. In his left hand he holds a *lituus*, a wand curving up at the lower end; the crescent-shaped hilt of a sword protrudes from his cloak. The figure stands on two rounded objects designated as mountains by a scale-pattern. Over the king's extended right hand is chiseled his name and full title in hieroglyphic symbols arranged as a cartouche (cf. relief No. 83 in the smaller Chamber B = Fig. 155): below at the center is the name – the hieroglyphic sign "tu" – which looks like a high boot lying on its back; above this there is the symbol of a bearded mountain god in a frilled skirt and a high pointed hat; both to the right and left is inscribed the title *labarna* (a dagger over a blossom), and framing this – at the far right and left – the insignia for "Great King" (a high cone under a volute); and above the entire sign floats a winged double sun.

Two deities in relief (Nos. 65-66) stand in poor preservation on the nose-like protrusion of the rock face just right of the entrance to Chamber A (cf. Fig. 142). A **male figure** in a high pointed hat sits opposite a **female figure** in a high rectangular headdress. Between them is a **table** or **sac-**

Fig. 149 Yazılıkaya. One of the demons (relief no. 68) at the entrance to Chamber B

rificial altar. The names above both figures begin with the sign for deity, but what follows is illegible.

This relief may have been related to the large fissure which penetrates deep into the rock to the right of it. Excavation within the cleft unfortunately proved unable to provide us with many clues to Hittite cult ritual.

A narrow channel through the rock provides entry into the smaller Chamber B. Two winged lion-headed demons in relief (Nos. 67-68) stand guard outside the passage (Fig. 149). With arms threateningly raised, they seem to be protecting the entrance.

Chamber B

The chamber, about 18 m long, is 4 m wide at the north end, narrowing to 2.5 m at the south (Fig. 150). The faces of the steeply rising high walls at the sides were left natural, without trimming or paring. The relief sculpture here is much better preserved because the chamber was partly filled with earth and remained unexcavated until the mid 19th century.

We assume that this chamber was a **memorial** or even the **sepulture** of the

Fig. 150   Chamber B at Yazılıkaya

Fig. 151   A Hittite statue base perhaps originally from Chamber B at Yazılıkaya

Great King Tudhaliya IV installed by his son Shupiluliuma II. Possibly a **statue** was erected here. The large **limestone block** by the entrance at the northern end of the chamber could well have been the base of it. A large basalt slab of the same dimensions, bearing the over-life-size feet of a statue, was found in the neighboring village of Yekbas/Evren and transported to the Boğazkale Museum garden in 1981 (Fig. 151). Judging from the size of the feet, the statue itself must have stood at least 3 m high.

On the wall immediately to the right of the entrance was carved a line of **gods of the Underworld** (relief Nos. 69-80; Figs. 152 and 155). Identical to the figures at the end of the procession of gods (relief Nos. 1-12) in the larger Chamber A,

Fig. 152 Chamber B at Yazılıkaya. Twelve gods of the Underworld (relief nos. 69-80)

they wear shirts, belts, short skirts and shoes curling up at the toe. They each carry a crescent-shaped sword flung over the shoulder, and the horned pointed hats that identify them as divinities.

The three reliefs described below adorn the wall opposite.

The God Sharrumma striding forward with the Great King Tudhaliya IV under his arm (relief No. 81; Figs. 153 and 155). The divinity Sharrumma, the patron of Tudhaliya IV, is depicted as an escort of the Great King (after his death?), who carries the same long curling wand (a *lituus*) as he does in Relief Number 64 in the main chamber, and is dressed the same, again wearing a long robe with a shawl, a rounded cap and shoes curling up at the

Fig. 153 Chamber B at Yazılıkaya. The Great King Tudhaliya IV in the embrace of the god Sharrumma (relief no. 81)

toe. Sharrumma, portrayed at a noticeably larger scale, wears a short skirt with a belt, and a twist of hair falls down his back. Both figures carry short swords with sickle-shaped hilts. Scharrumma's left arm is thrown around the King's shoulders to grasp the wrist of his upraised right hand. Behind the tall horned hat of the god appears a cartouche with the name and titles of the king. At the far right the sign for "hero" has been added here; the insignia also differs from those of the king here in relief No. 83 and relief No. 64 in the main chamber in that the ideogram for "mountain god" replaces the pictorial representations. With these three reliefs Great King Tudhaliya IV is the sole human being represented among the gods in the whole of the two chambers.

The Sword God, or the god Nergal of the Underworld (relief No. 82; Figs. 154-155). This most unusual iconography depicts an upright sword with the pommel on the hilt above fashioned into a male head wearing the tall horned and pointed hat of the gods. He wears a ring in his ear, and his hair falls down the back of his neck. In place of arms and shoulders are the foreparts of two crouching lions, facing outwards. The hilt itself is formed by two lions with teeth bared, portrayed vertically as if creeping down the two sides. Below the hilt is a vertically ribbed blade, narrowing towards the point which is not depicted; there might have been a podium against the rock face here.

Cartouche with the name and title of the Great King Tudhaliya IV (relief No. 83; Fig. 155). This cartouche is for the greatest part like that next to the large relief of the King in Chamber A (relief No. 64). Under a

Fig. 154 Chamber B at Yazılıkaya. The "Sword God", Nergal of the Underworld (relief no. 82)

69   70   71   72   73   74   75   76

81

Fig. 155 Drawing of the reliefs of Chamber B at Yazılıkaya

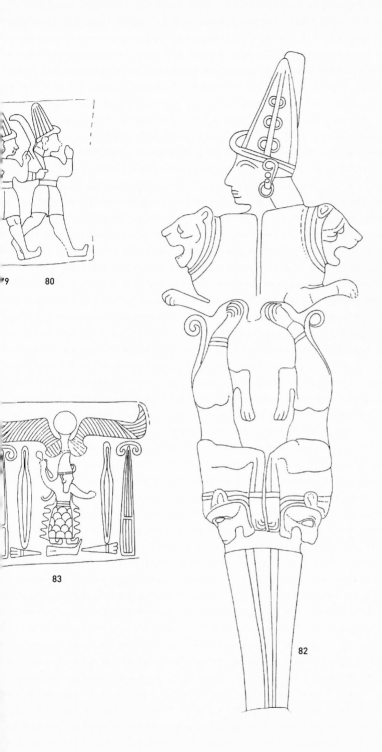

9   80

83

82

winged sun we see the name in the center; it is composed of the hieroglyphic sign for "tu" (which resembles a high boot lying heel downward) under a pictogram of a bearded mountain god wearing a ruffled skirt and high hat and holding a mace in his raised right hand; to both the left and the right then comes the symbol for "labarna" (a dagger above a blossom); and finally at the exterior left and right, the title "Great King" (a high cone under a volute). This cartouche may have been meant to identify the cult statue that hypothetically stood at the north end of the chamber.

In the rock face at the back of the room there are three **deep niches** (Fig. 153) where offerings might have been placed.

Assuming that the cult statue once stood at the north end of the chamber, towards which the reliefs face as well, one might think that the **original entrance** should have been in the southern part of the chamber. However, what must have been a natural opening in the side here was obstructed already in Hittite times by the large blocks you see in place today.

The Hittites, their forerunners and their followers

A brief history of Hattusha/ Boğazköy over the millennia.

This chapter attempts to present a background for your visit to Hattusha/Boğazköy. In case the ruins awaken still further curiosity, a bibliographic appendix lists sources with more detailed information.

The Landscape. Hattusha, or Boğazköy, lies in northern Central Anatolia, just at the north edge of the ancient region of Cappadocia. Within a dry continental climatic zone, we see scant steppe-vegetation; over some large areas there is scarcely a tree in sight. The winters are long and cold; the summers relatively short,

Fig. 156 Winter in Hattusha is cold and long

but hot. This was not always the case, however; in earlier times the climate was more moist, with lesser extremes in temperature. Bordering the central steppe of Cappadocia (to the south of Yozgat) were more temperate regions – most particularly to the north – with dense vegetation and forests. The denser plant cover prevented erosion and raised the level of the ground water, which again benefited the vegetation. Conditions were more suitable for agriculture and husbandry than today, and the woods sheltered a large variety of wild game.

Very few traces from the Paleolithic and Mesolithic periods – when man was still a wandering hunter and gatherer – have been discovered in northern Anatolia. Even from the Neolithic period, when man had begun to settle down to a livelihood of raising his own crops and animals, there is not much more evidence of his populating this region. The early farming societies apparently did not find the wooded, mountainous landscape to their liking. The open meadows and milder climates to the south must have been more attractive, for that is where the first developed farming communities sprang up; of these, Çatal Hüyük near Çumra in the Konya Plain is perhaps the best known.

Before the Hittites: the autochthonous Anatolians *(5th -3rd millennia BC)*

The first "settling in" around Boğazköy took place in the 5th millennium BC during the **Chalcolithic period**, when small widely scattered hamlets appeared most particularly on mountain slopes and rocky outcroppings. Such a small settlement on the heights of the Büyükkaya ridge represents the earliest known inhabitancy

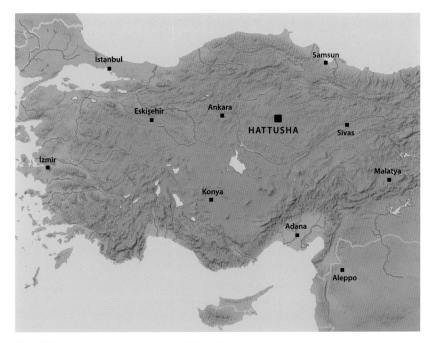

Fig. 157 Map of western and central Anatolia

within the Hattusha city limits. A contemporary settlement has also been found near Yarıkkaya, some two kilometers NE of Hattusha; the finds are on display at the Boğazkale Museum.

In the following millennia settlement in this wooded landscape of northern Anatolia increased very slowly. It was first in the 3rd millennium BC – during the **Early Bronze Age** – that coherent zones of habitation, settlements that actively traded with one another, developed and founded the basis for advancement in society. Small settlements grew into political and religious centers, wielding their influence over larger and larger dominions. The discovery and development of the mineral sources in northern Anatolia is believed to have been one of the stimulating factors.

One thriving center was located at Alaca Höyük, only 25 km from Hattusha/Boğazköy. The astoundingly rich chamber tombs (known as the Royal Graves) discovered at Alaca Höyük yielded elegantly fashioned weapons, jewelry, and sculpture, as well as implements and vessels of gold, silver, electron, bronze – and even iron – from a period as early as 2400-2200 BC. (The original finds are on display in the Museum of Anatolian Civilzations in Ankara, reproductions in the Museum of Alaca Höyük.) The inhabitants of the site were **Hatti**, the natives of north and Central Anatolia and the predecessors of the Hittites in this region.

Soon there was a Hattian settlement at Boğazköy as well, and this habitation, founded towards the end of the Early Bronze Age, marked the beginning of **continuous occupation at the site.**

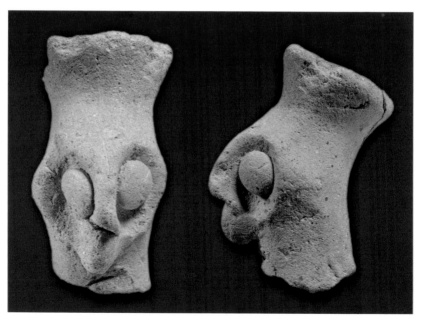

Fig. 158 Early Bronze Age figurine head from Büyükkaya

Remnants of the Hattian settlement have been located under the fill of the Hittite Lower City. During this period there was also occupation on the high ridges of Büyükkaya and Büyükkale, with evidence even of fortification walls.

Hattush and the Assyrian Trade Colonies
(ca. 2000-1700 BC)

During the Middle Bronze Age the Hattian occupation grew into a city of such significance that a **Karum** was established here in the 19th and 18th centuries BC – a **trading post of Assyrian merchants** who had come from Assur (in the middle Tigris valley, now a part of northern Iraq) to procure natural resources such as copper, silver, gold and precious stones. Long caravans of donkeys transported these materials to Mesopotamia, where they loaded Mesopotamian goods for exchange – including tin, garments and fabric – and set out on the return journey. Along their route the Assyrian merchants also dealt in local Anatolian products; the whole of eastern Anatolia was enmeshed in the net of their routes, knotted together by their trade colonies. In Central Anatolia they established such colonies at several centers of Hattian rule. The Assyrian traders and their families lived in separate residential quarters; they enjoyed the protection of their Hattian lords and paid taxes in return. The center of their network was located in Kanesh/Nesha (at the site of Kültepe near Kayseri).

It was these Assyrian traders who first introduced writing to Anatolia, for business could hardly be transacted without documentation. Purchases and sales, orders, credits, and exchanges were all recorded in Akkadian cuneiform writing on clay tablets.

On these tablets the name of the city was written as well; Boğazköy was still – or already, we had better say – **Hattush**.

During this era, known as the Karum period, fortifications were laid out on Büyükkale. It would seem that the rulers of Hattush resided there; the rest of the Hattian settlement stretched from the slope below Büyükkale to the area where the Great Temple of the Hittites was later erected. The Karum of the Assyrian traders lay just to the north. Both the settlement and the Karum must also have been fortified against enemy attacks.

During these first centuries of the 2nd millennium BC there appears to have been frequent strife in Central Anatolia between the local Hattian rulers and the immigrant Hittite groups who were anxious to consolidate their power. The

0   1 cm.

Fig. 159
A double-headed eagle
on a stamp seal from
the Karum period,
(19th -18th centuries BC)

ruins excavated demonstrate that the city of Hattush was burned down in a great conflagration around 1700 BC. The destruction of the city was even inscribed in cuneiform; a King Anitta of Kushar reports that he has defeated King Piyushti of Hattush and destroyed his city. "At night I took the city by force; I have sown weeds in its place. Should any king after me attempt to resettle Hattush", he wrote, "may the Weathergod of Heaven strike him down". Anitta chose the city of Kanesh/Nesha, some 160 km to the south-east and already quite influential as the center of the Assyrian trade colonies, as his capital.

We do not know how long Anitta's curse on the city of Hattush was respected, but the advantages of the site and the many springs there were certainly enough to have attracted settlers relatively soon. By the second half of the 17th century BC the temptation had obviously become overwhelming, for a Hittite king had indeed chosen the site as his residence and capital. The Hattian Hattush was now the **Hittite Hattusha.**

The Period of the Old Hittite Kingdom
(ca. 1650/1600 - 1400/1350 BC)

Unfortunately very little is known about the origins of the Hittites. Their language belongs to the **Indo-European** family, and it is generally assumed that they immigrated into Central Anatolia via the Caucasus sometime during the second half of the 3rd millennium BC. To ascribe any date to their arrival is difficult, particularly because there is evidence neither of violent invasion nor of massive population shift. They must have moved into Anatolia little by little, in small groups that mingled to some extent with the autochthonous Hattian population. Other Indo-Europeans were also drifting into Anatolia at around this time: the Luvians into the south and west, and the Palaians into the north and northwest.

The Hittites retained the name Hatti as the designation for their land. Their language, however, they called Neshian after the town of Kanish/Nesha, mentioned above. The first king in

Hattusha/Boğazköy came – like Anitta – from Kushar, a city still awaiting rediscovery. Nonetheless he took the name of Hattushili, or "one from Hattusha". During his reign cuneiform writing was introduced once again; it had fallen out of use with the breakdown of the Assyrian trade network. Writing developed into a tradition, leaving behind a veritable information bank in the archives of clay tablets; these include official Hittite correspondence and contracts, as well as legal codes, procedures for cult ceremony, oracular prophecies and literature of the ancient Near East. Although the 33,000 or so clay tablet pieces recovered from 1906 onwards in the archives of Hattusha form the main corpus, archives have since appeared at other Hittite centers in Anatolia: Tabigga/Maşat Höyük (Tokat province), Shapinuwa/Ortaköy (Çorum province) and Sarissa/Kuşaklı (Sivas province).

The Great King Hattushili I **built an empire** through the military campaigns he directed at sites in Central Anatolia and further south over the Taurus Mountains into northern Syria. His successor Murshili continued his efforts to the south in hopes of vanquishing the city-states in Syria and gaining control of the trade routes to Mesopotamia. Aleppo fell into the hands of the Hittites, and the army pressed onward as far as Babylon (as the crow flies, 1,200 km from Hattusha!), where it toppled the dynasty of Hammurabi. A period of unrest followed the murder of Murshili, and in these troubled times the lands south of the Taurus as well as distant regions in the south and east of Anatolia were soon snatched from Hittite control by the Hurrian Kingdom of the Mitanni.

It would make too long a diversion to follow all the waning and waxing of Hittite power over the following decades of

Fig. 160 A stylus of wood or metal was used to incise the cuneiform signs in the moist clay

Anatolian history. The armies remained active in many regions and advanced again to Aleppo in the north of Syria. Only too often would the conquered cities and states, adopted as tax-paying vassals, soon become unfaithful. Meanwhile, the attacks of marauding Kashkan tribes living in the mountains of north-Central Anatolia had become a direct threat to the Hittite capital. One cuneiform text from around 1400 BC during the reign of the Great King Tudhaliya III reports that ". . . Hattusha, the city, was burned to the ground and only [. . .] and the Heshti-House of [. . .] remained standing". By the end of this period the domain under direct Hittite control had shrunk once more to limits within the Central Anatolia plateau and the city found itself in a period of deep crisis.

The Old Hittite city comprised the same area as that of its Hattian predecessor; on the high ridge of Büyükkale was the residence of the Great King, and the city lay on the slope below to the northwest, reaching to the valley below and protected to the west by a massive fortification wall. It would appear that the northern section of the settlement and the rocky crest of Büyükkaya were also enclosed by fortifications and incorporated into the city. The enclosed city would then have boasted dimensions of approximately 0.9x1.2 km, and there may well have been further residential quarters just outside the city walls.

The Period of the Hittite Empire
(ca. 1400/1350 - 1180 BC)

With the Great King Shupiluliuma I coming into power, the Hittites again had a ruler who was able to lead their sadly weakened and diminished realm to a new magnitude. They finally managed to rupture the power of the Mitanni empire, the mighty opponent in the Tigris and Euphrates basin (today the southeast of Turkey and the northern parts of Syria and Iraq). With Hittite territory now bordering directly on the northernmost province of Pharaonic Egypt, there was soon strife between these two great powers. They came face to face in the famous **Battle of Khadesh** on the Orontes (near Homs in Syria) in ca.1274 BC, when the army of the Great King Muwattalli II pitched against that of the Pharaoh Ramses II. The battle ended in a draw, and in the development of a relationship between the two lands that led within a few years to a peace treaty which staunchly endured throughout the rest of the Hittite Empire period. (In the New York Headquarters of the United Nations an enlarged copy of a

Fig. 161 Two cult vessels from Büyükkale (14th century BC). They probably represent the celestial bulls Hurri and Sheri, attendants of the storm god Teshub

clay tablet from Hattusha setting out the conditions of the agreement hangs on the wall as an example of one of the earliest international peace treaties in the world).

During the reign of Muwattalli, Hattusha lost its role as the capital for a short while when the King moved his residency to Tarhuntasha, a city in the southwest – another site still awaiting discovery. It was not long before his successor, Murshili III, returned to Hattusha, only to be quickly deposed by his uncle

Hattushili III. It was under this ruler and his son Tudhaliya IV. that the city went through a time of revival; many of the structures visible today stem from this period. Also the area of the Upper City, the area south of the Old City (= Lower City), received much attention. This area had been integrated into the city already considerably earlier, but large parts of the fortification wall which we see here today perhaps were built or rebuilt during this late period. Within the wall, new and large structures were built, especially temples. In addition, the Royal Citadel was completely renovated into a large palace with colonnaded stoas, residences, and storage facilities as well as an audience- or reception hall. Finally, then, Tudhaliya IV is also credited with having brought the rock sanctuary at Yazılıkaya to its ultimate arrangement. Hattusha was, after all, not only the political center of the Hittite

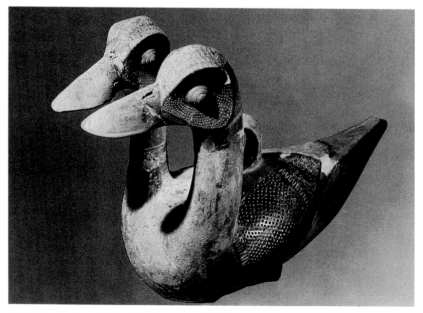

Fig. 162 Two-headed duck (14th century BC) from the Lower City of Hattusha

Fig. 163 Bronze tablet with the cuneiform text of a treaty between the Great King
Tudhaliya IV of Hattusha and King Kurunta of Tarhuntasha (2nd half of the
13th century BC)

state, but the **religious center** of the land as well – residence of "the Thousand Gods of the Hatti-Land".

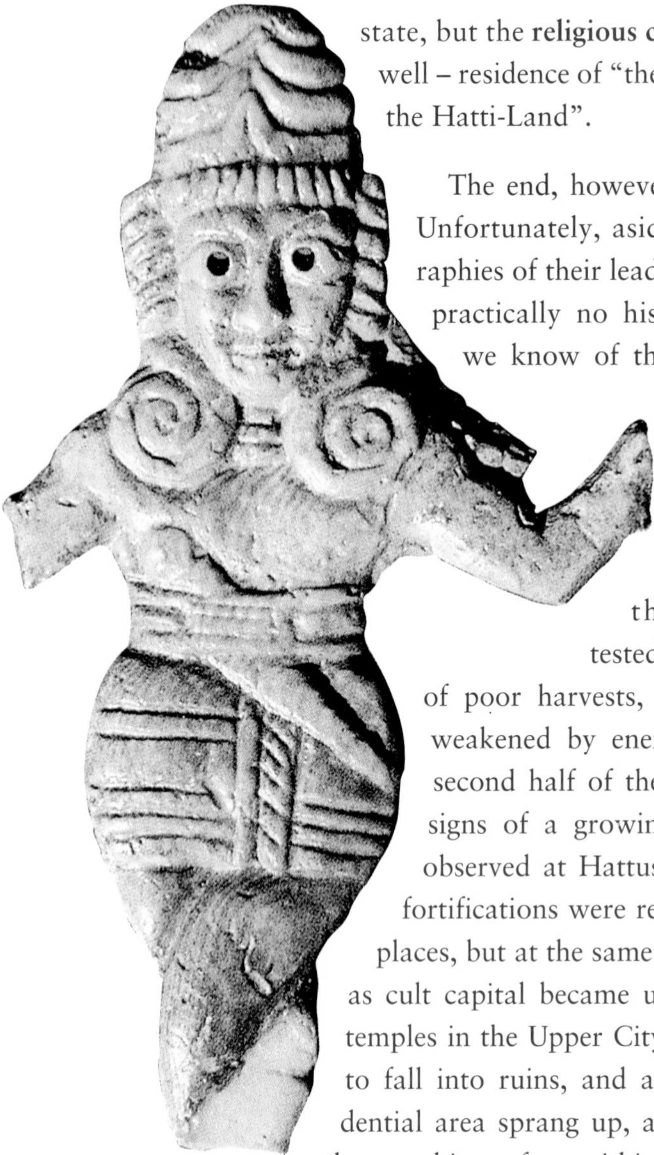

The end, however, was not far off. Unfortunately, aside from some biographies of their leaders, the Hittites left practically no historical texts; what we know of the final decline has been pieced together, a mosaic of bits and pieces of information: succession to the throne was contested, there were years of poor harvests, and the state was weakened by enemy attacks. In the second half of the 13th century BC, signs of a growing pressure can be observed at Hattusha: apparently the fortifications were reinforced in various places, but at the same time the cities' role as cult capital became under threat. Many temples in the Upper City had been allowed to fall into ruins, and among these a residential area sprang up, apparently to house those seeking refuge within the city walls.

Fig. 164
Ivory statuette of a dancing (?)
god from Temple 7
(13th century BC)

Thus the great empire came to an end, bringing with it the close of the Bronze Age in Central Anatolia. It was indeed a time of unrest throughout the whole of the Mediterranean region, the era when the coastal populations were suffering piratical attacks at the hands of the so-called Sea Peoples. Entire populations were migrating from one place to another, and in Central Anatolia there was no one to take over the empire structured by the Hittites; the scant population left in the region retreated into a pastoral, partially nomadic way of life.

The End of the Capital City Hattusha
(ca. 1200/1180 BC)

With the decline of its great empire, the capital lost its influence and thereby also its role as a political, economic and religious center. Little by little its residents drifted away and certainly the last known Hittite king, the Great King Shupiluliuma II, son of Tudhaliya IV, did not remain in Hattusha to the bitter end. He may well have moved his court elsewhere, thus sealing the fate of the city.

Various complexes of the Empire period – the royal palace, certain temples, and stretches of the fortification walls among them – reveal signs of a fiery destruction. Perhaps part of this devastation can be attributed to the hands of an enemy. When the invaders entered the city, however, they must have found it nearly deserted, for the rooms destroyed by the fire had already been virtually cleared of their contents. Only what was worthless or stationary had been left behind. To the former category belong the records, the documents on file in the clay tablet archives; to the second, furnishings such as the huge storage vessels in the temple magazines.

Until very recently we were dependent entirely on speculation as to who was responsible for the final desertion of the Hittite city. No trace whatever had been found of invaders who took over the site and settled here. It was assumed that the Kashkans, the restless northern neighbors of the Hittites, had dealt the dying city the fatal blow. Finally in 1996 the small settlement of a foreign population was discovered on the ridge of Büyükkaya. These people, who were by no means Hittites, settled down here after the desertion of the city. With them begins the Iron Age history of the site.

The Iron Age: "the Dark Ages" and the Period of the Phrygians and Persians
(ca. 1180 - 334 BC)

The first phase of the Iron Age in Central Anatolia was often spoken of as the Dark Ages because there were almost no traces testifying to inhabitancy over the first 300 years following the demise of the Hittite Empire. Recently, however, settlements – including that on Büyükkaya in the northeast of the city Hattusha/Boğazköy – have been introduced to the literature. The inhabitants of these settlements lacked much of what the Hittites had taken for granted. They shaped their pottery by hand, for example, without aid of the potter's wheel, which had enabled mass production of pottery in the Hittite community. Their primitive dwellings had nothing in common with the architecture

Fig. 165
This vessel from the
middle phases of the
Iron Age (8th century BC)
from Alishar Höyük
is painted with stylized
animals

of the Hittites, and writ-ing was unknown to them. With a material culture resembling that of their Early and Middle Bronze Age ancestors, they obviously represent native (northern) Anatolian inhabitants who moved in to settle in the former heartland of the Hittites after the fall of the empire. There is thus no reason they could not have been the Kashkans mentioned above. They came to Hattusha not as conquerers, but as squatters; there were certainly many things useful to them to be found in the ruins.

Traces of this "Dark Age" settlement of the early Iron Age are by no means limited only to the settlement on Büyükkaya; evidence of these people has been found in the Lower City near the House on the Slope, on the rocky platform of Büyükkale and in the area of Temple 7 in the Upper City. At the beginning of the middle Iron Age in the 9th century BC, their presence on Büyük-kale developed into a sizable settlement incorporating the whole of the rocky outcropping. By the 8th century, the community had spread out, inhabiting parts of the Lower City and the citadel on Büyükkale. In the early- to mid-7th century the settlers fortified Büyükkale (Fig. 166); at the same time, there was a marked decrease in the population settled in the Lower City. Büyükkaya was deserted as well. This may have been a response to invasions of the Cimmerians, who pushed their way from the steppes of Eurasia into Central Anatolia around 700/680 BC, breaking up the Phrygian realm of King Midas. Besides the fortified citadel on Büyükkale, which was very densely built up, the Southern Citadel was established, as well as residential areas above the East Ponds and near Nişantaş.

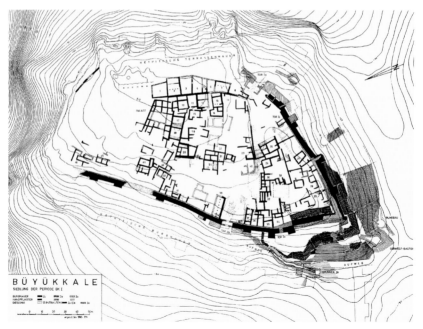

Fig. 166 Plan of the mid-Iron Age fortress (7th-6th centuries BC) on Büyükkale (P. Neve)

Fig. 167 Statue of the goddess Cybele from the Southeast
Gate of the Iron Age fortress on Büyükkale

This middle- and late Iron Age settlement is traditionally ter-
med **"Phrygian"** because it shares many features in common with
sites within the Phrygian nuclear zone in western Anatolia. Simi-
larities include the architecture as well as the material culture. The
cult of the Phrygian mother-goddess Cybele is also attested here;
a lovely depiction of Cybele was found at the Level-Ia southeast
gate at Büyükkale (Fig. 167). Potsherds with symbols of Phrygian

script scratched upon them supply further proof of connections with the west, as do a few pieces of original East-Greek imported wares. The Central Anatolian and northern Cappadocian settlements had obviously developed close ties with the western regions of Central Anatolia during this period, but any sizable migration of Phrygians into this area is highly unlikely. Unfortunately we do not know the name of the Iron Age settlement here, but we can probably rule out the earlier suggestion of Pteria, for that city has since been tentatively located at Mount Kerkenes, some 40 km southeast of Hattusha/Boğazköy.

In 585 BC all the Central Anatolian land east of the river Kızılırmak (the Halys of antiquity) fell into the hands of the Iranian **Medes**, and still later, into the hands of the Persian **Achaemenids**. These "Persian times", however, appear not to have had much effect on the development of settlement here in Hattusha/Boğazköy; tradition carried on as before. Although in the 5th century BC the site seems to have lost significance, it nevertheless remained inhabited.

The Hellenistic/Galatian and Roman/ Byzantine Periods

(ca. 334 BC - 1071 AD)

The Asian expedition of Alexander the Great marks the beginnings of the Hellenistic period in Asia Minor. Although at first it had little impact on Central Anatolia, in the first half of the 3rd century BC Celtic **Galatian** emigrants from central Europe settled here. The site of Tavium near the village Büyük Nefesköy some 20 km south of Boğazköy became the seat of the Trokmer clan, who took the land around Hattusha/Boğazköy under their control. Büyükkale once again became a fortified citadel, and a small village occupied part of what had been the Lower City. The painted pottery characteristic of the Galatians was recovered here, as well as vessels imported from the Hellenistic cities along the west coast.

In 25 BC the lands of the Trokmer came under the administration of the **Romans**, who built a paved road from Tavium northwards (possibly to Amasya) in the first century AD. The road ran behind the mountain ridge west of Hattusha/Boğazköy and then crossed the valley of the Budaközü stream near the village of Yekbas/Evren a few kilometers north of Boğazkale. Evidence of the Roman presence within the area of the city from this and the following centuries includes scattered building remains, graves, and traces of quarrying.

Although not many remains from the early Byzantine period have been recognized, in **middle Byzantine times** there was a 10th-through 11th century village in the area of the Upper City, to the north of the Hittite Temple District. (Several small churches and a large cemetery here, as well as various farmsteads have been excavated and partially restored.) The Hittite complex on the rocks of Sarıkale was renovated and enclosed by a fortification wall at this time, most probably to serve as the residence for the local dignitaries. Byzantine remains are found in the Lower City as well. The most noticeable is the apse of a church cut into the rock called Mihraplıkaya (= rock with a prayer-niche) (General Plan: No. 36; Fig. 169).

A secure date for the Byzantine settlement is given by the coins recovered there. The latest coins, from the late 11th century, tell us when the settlement was deserted. This date corresponds with the Battle of Malazgirt on the shores of Lake Van in 1071. It was then under the ruler Emperor Romanos IV that the Byzantines lost their control over vast areas of Anatolia to the Seljuk Sultan Alpaslan.

Fig. 168 Byzantine Church in the Upper City

Fig. 169 Mihraplıkaya in the Lower City: the apse of a Byzantine church hewn into the rock

Fig. 170 Boğazkale

Turkish Settlement at Boğazköy/Boğazkale

Over the next few centuries, settlement in the area seems to have been quite sparse. This changed in the 16th century when a group of the Türkmen clan known as the Dülkadiroğlu came from Maraş to resettle here. Their first settlement was at Yekbas, three kilometers to the north; it was towards the end of the 17th century that they moved here and erected the Konak (the residence of the most important) and their village just at the foot of the former Hittite capital. The locality was then known as Boğazköy (= gorge village), which was later changed to Boğazkale (= gorge fortress). It is today a local administrative center in the Province of Çorum.

Fig. 171 The excavation team of Hattusha in 1995

The excavation

Many find participation in an archaeological excavation rather like the Labor of Sisyphus. Excavation does indeed require much patience, and from time to time exacting work requires fine trowling and the use of a putty-knife or paintbrush – or even dental tools. Everyday tasks, however, deal more often with the removal of the quantities of earth and debris which have buried the ruins of the fortification walls, buildings and ponds over the past few thousand years. Picks, shovels and wheelbarrows come into play for this more laborious work. Not only in "digging" itself, but in measuring, drawing and restoring as well, the men of Boğazkale have proved untiring. Some of them are third – or fourth – generation staff, and their experience has played an appreciable role in investigating the past at this site.

The Discovery and Excavation of Boğazköy/ Hattusha

1834   On July 28 Charles Texier discovers the ruins of Hattusha. Believing he has found Pteria, a city of the Medes, he makes drawings of reliefs at Yazılıkaya and some of the city ruins, and prepares a rough plan of the city.

1836   William J. Hamilton makes a day's excursion to Hattusha, where he does various drawing, including a plan of Temple 1. He is convinced that the ruins represent the Galatian/Roman city Tavium.

1858   Heinrich Barth and Andreas D. Mordtmann senior make drawings of the ruins of Temple 1 and have the reliefs in the smaller Chamber B at Yazılıkaya cleared.

1861   Georges Perrot, Edmont Guillaume and Jules Delbet prepare more accurate drawings of the Yazılıkaya relief sculpture, and publish the first photographs of Yazılıkaya, Yenicekale and the Nişantaş inscription.

1864   Henry J. van Lennep prepares new drawings of Yazılıkaya.

1882   Karl Humann prepares a topographic plan and takes plaster molds of many of the Yazılıkaya reliefs.

1893-94 Ernest Chantre opens exploratory trenches in the Great Temple, on Büyükkale and in Yazılıkaya. He publishes the first cuneiform tablets from Hattusha.

1906   Hugo Winckler and Theodor Makridi begin excavating on Büyük-kale on behalf of the Ottoman Museum in Istanbul and make sondages in various other places. 2500 fragments of cuneiform tablets recovered here first identify the city as the Hittite capital Hattusha.

1907   Continuation of the excavations under participation of the German Archaeological Institute and the German Oriental Society; field directors include Otto Puchstein as well as Winckler and Makridi. The first real documentation of the ruins, complete with many plans and photos, is compiled and a more accurate topographic map prepared.

1911-12 Winckler and Makridi conduct shorter excavation campaigns.

1915   With the aid of the cuneiform tablets from Boğazköy, Bedrich Hrozny is able to decipher the Hittite language.

1931-39 and 1952 to the present

The German Archaeological Institute, for many years with the cooperation of the German Oriental Society as well, conducts excavations; the successive directors have been Kurt Bittel (through 1977), Peter Neve (1978-1993), Jürgen Seeher (1994-2005) and Andreas Schachner. Nearly all the remains of the Hittite Royal Citadel on Büyükkale have been cleared, and large-scale excavation has exposed wide areas of the settlement in the Lower City, the Great Temple, the temple precinct in the Upper City and its surroundings, as well as on the high spur of Büyükkaya. Since 2009, excavation concentrates in the area of the Lower City. Excavation on a smaller scale has been carried out in various other locations within the city and in the immediate surroundings, as well as in the rock sanctuary of Yazılıkaya.

Acknowledgements (1ˢᵗ Edition, 1999)

This guidebook represents the cooperative efforts of many. Uğurhan Betin is responsible for most of the reconstruction drawings; his drawings Figures 23 and 137, as well as the map Figure 157 have been reproduced with the permission of ATLAS Dergisi. Ulf Schoop has provided us with the drawing in Figure 4 and page 33. The individual plans have been adapted from the topographical plan of Hans P. Birk (= the general plan at the back of the guide). The photographs have been taken from the Boğazköy Archives; most of those used were taken by Murat Can or Dieter Johannes. Figs. 14, 15, 57, 81, 88, 100 and 124, have been provided by Peter Oszvald. The aerial shot (Fig. 62) was taken by Hakan Öge on a daring flight in a motorized hang-glider. The illustrations of a few certain finds have been taken from other publications: Figures 70, 161 and 162 from K. Bittel, Die Hethiter (C.H. Beck, 1976); Figure 164 from P. Neve, Hattusa, Stadt der Götter und Tempel (Ph. von Zabern, 1996); and Figure 165 from the Catalogue of the Tokyo exhibition Land of Civilizations, Turkey (1985). The English version was translated by Jean D. Carpenter Efe, and the Turkish by Ümit Öztürk and Ayşe Baykal-Seeher; she deserves credit for a variety of other assistance with the preparation of the book as well.

The publication of the guide has been financed through private contributions, including those of Margo T. Tytus, Martha W. Jones, Sara W. Headley, Patricia P. Whitaker, Ayşe S. Gonzales and Nurettin Siago. The efforts of Hülya Tokmak, Ayşe Orhun and Ahmet Boratav of the publishing house Ege Yayınları have successfully and promptly produced a work of high quality.

Here I wish to express my appreciation to those mentioned above; with their help in this project, they have all contributed to spreading our knowledge of Hattusha and the Hittites.

Select Bibliography

Hattusha

Bittel, K.   *Hattuscha. Hauptstadt der Hethiter*
                    (DuMont, Köln 1983)

Bittel, K.   *Hattusha. The Capital of the Hittites*
                    (Oxford University Press, New York 1970)

Neve, P.   *Hattuscha - Information*
                    (Arkeoloji ve Sanat Yayınları, İstanbul 1985)

Neve, P.   *Ḫattuša – Stadt der Götter und Tempel*
                    (Philipp von Zabern, Mainz 1996)

Schachner, A.   *Hattuscha – Auf den Spuren der sagenhaften
                    Hauptstadt der Hethiter*
                    (C.H. Beck Verlag München 2011)

Seeher, J.   *A Mudbrick City Wall at Hattusa. Diary of a
                    Reconstruction*
                    (Ege Yayınları Istanbul 2007)

Seeher, J.   *Gods Carved in Stone. The Hittite Rock Sanctuary
                    of Yazılıkaya*
                    (Ege Yayınları Istanbul 2011)

Hittites and History of Anatolia

Akurgal, E.   *Hatti ve Hitit Uygarlıkları*
                    (Yaşar Eğitim ve Kültür Vakfı, Izmir 1995)

Akurgal, E.   Anadolu Kültür Tarihi
                    (TÜBİTAK Popüler Bilim Kitapları, Ankara 1998)

Alp, S.   *Hitit Çağında Anadolu*
                    (TÜBİTAK Popüler Bilim Kitapları, Ankara 2001)

Bittel, K.   *Die Hethiter* (Beck, München 1976)

Bittel, K.   *Les Hittites* (Gallimard, Paris 1976)

Brandau, B. – H. Schickert
                    Hethiter. Die unbekannte Weltmacht
                    (Piper, München 2001)

Bryce, T.   *The Kingdom of the Hittites*
(University Press, Oxford 2005)

Bryce, T.   *Life and Society in the Hittite World*
(University Press, Oxford 2004)

Collins B.J.   *The Hittites and Their World* (Brill, Leiden/Boston 2008)

Darga, M.   *Hitit Sanatı* (Akbank Yayınları, Istanbul 1992)

De Martino, S.   *Gli Ittiti* (Carocci, Roma 2003)

Imparati, F.   *La civiltà degli Ittiti. Caratteri e problemi,* in: Bucci, O.
(ed.), Antichi popoli indoeuropei (Roma 1993) 367-456.

Klengel, H.   *Geschichte des hethitischen Reiches* (Brill, Leiden-Boston-
Köln 1999)

Klinger, J.   *Die Hethiter* (C.H. Beck Verlag München 2007)

Klock – Fontanille, I.
Les Hittites (Presses Universitaires de France 1998)

MacQueen, J.G. *The Hittites and their Contemporaries in Asia Minor*
(Thames & Hudson, London 1996)

MacQueen, J.G. *Gli Ittiti, un Impero sugli Altipiani* (Roma 1990)

Visit the Hattusha homepage at
www.hattuscha.de

The German Institute of Archaeology is on the Internet at
www.dainst.org

up-to-date information on the excavations at Hattusha is
also available at
www.dainst.org/hattusa

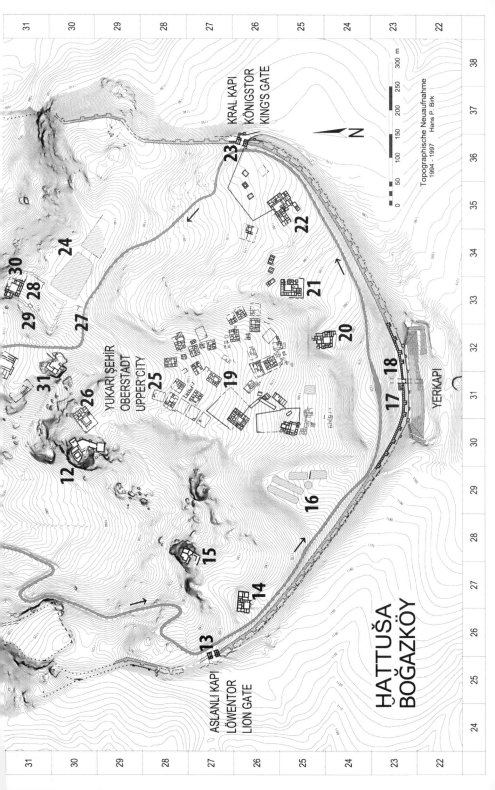

HATTUŠA
BOĞAZKÖY

ASLANLI KAPI
LÖWENTOR
LION GATE

KRAL KAPI
KÖNIGSTOR
KING'S GATE

YUKARI ŞEHİR
OBERSTADT
UPPER CITY

YERKAPI

Topographische Neuaufnahme
1994 - 1997   Hans P. Birk

N

0   50   100   150   200   250   300 m

ALSO AVAILABLE